Spiritual Heart Attack

to Recovery

By Phyllis Kilgore

P.O. Box 405
Swiftwater, PA 18370
(973) 348-5067
sspublishingcompany@gmail.com
www.sharsheypublishingcompany.com

Copyright © 2019 Phyllis Kilgore
ISBN: 13: 978-0-9997922-6-1
ISBN: 10: 0-9997922-6-1
Publisher: Shar- Shey Publishing Company LLC
Book Cover Designed by: Miss Web Designer
Edited by: ATW Editing

All rights reserved. No part of this book may be reproduced or transmitted in any form or by any means, electronic or mechanical, including photocopying, recording, or by any information storage and retrieval system, without permission in writing from the copyright owner. This book was printed in the United States of America.

TABLE of CONTENTS

Acknowledgments

Introduction

Chapter One:
The Natural Heart vs. The Spiritual Heart

Chapter Two:
Biblical Medical Procedures for Healing & God's Word for Healing

Chapter Three:
The Meaning of Disease in the Natural & Spiritual Heart

Chapter Four:
Examining the Spiritual Heart

Chapter Five:
Spiritual Heart Malfunction

Chapter Six:
The Diagnosing & Prognosing of a Spiritual Heart

Chapter Seven:
Methods to Treating an Affected Spiritual Heart

Chapter Eight:
The Causes of Spiritual Heart Murmur

Chapter Nine:
The Irregularities of a Spiritual Heart

Chapter Ten:
How to Recognize a Doubtful Spiritual Heart

Chapter Eleven:
How a Spiritual Unbelieving Heart Occurs

Chapter Twelve:
How Spiritual Hard Heart Occurs

Chapter Thirteen:
How a Spiritual Deceitful Heart Happens

Chapter Fourteen:
What Occurs in a Spiritual Doubtful Heart

Chapter Fifteen:
The Affects of an Uncircumcised Spiritual Heart

Chapter Sixteen:
How a Spiritual Heart Attack Happens

Chapter Seventeen:
How to Receive a Spiritual Heart Transplant

Chapter Eighteen:
What Happens When Spiritual Heart Failure Occurs

Chapter Nineteen:
Resuscitation of a Spiritual Heart

Chapter Twenty:
Recovering from a Spiritual Heart Attack

Chapter Twenty-One:
The Keys to Recovering and Keeping a Spiritual Heart

Chapter Twenty-Two:
How the Word Works in Our Spiritual Hearts

Chapter Twenty-Three:
Confessing God's Word is Good Medication

Chapter Twenty-Four:
God Has Called Each of Us for His Purpose

Chapter Twenty-Five:
The Spiritual Heart and the Power in Prayer

Chapter Twenty-Six:
The Spiritual Heart Hears by the Word of God

ACKNOWLEDGMENTS

First, giving honor to God for inspiring me to experience a spiritual heart ailment to know he is able to heal, revive, and resuscitate my spiritual heart back to function in life's journey to help me to assist others who have lost children or anything that has caused a broken heart. I thank God for Dawn Pagan, an encourager that caused me to complete this assignment, Deb Wilkerson for copying and emailing the manuscript and anything to help. Donna Page Riley, who helped to format the chapters, and Elizabeth Bailey for encouraging and teaching me to stand on the word and prayer.

Phyllis Kilgore

INTRODUCTION

This book came about through the inspiration of the Holy Spirit, through Revelation knowledge. Experiencing the death of three of my five children caused me to be hurt and some depression. One day while in prayer, the Lord allowed me to see I had experienced a spiritual heart condition that was affecting my life. This is where the title of this book came from, Spiritual Heart Attack To Recovery, because God, through prayer and his word, began working healing in my spiritual heart that worked in healing my natural mind, and my depression left me. Each of us will experience some type of spiritual heart ailment that will affect us in every area of our lives but will comfort and heal us as we seek his help.

Chapter One

THE NATURAL HEART VS THE SPIRITUAL HEART

Introduction of the Natural and Spiritual Hearts

What is the natural heart? We have in our bodies a hollow muscle in the center of our chest known as the natural or physical heart; this muscular organ pumps blood throughout our bodies by contracting and expanding. The heart carries blood throughout the various parts of our bodies; this is called circulation.

The heart is a very important part of our physical makeup, because it is the center of life. If the blood doesn't flow properly to the heart, it will cause the heart to malfunction. These malfunctions will cause many problems to the heart, resulting in heart block, heart murmur, heart disease, irregular heartbeat, heart attack, and heart failure leading to physical death. Any of these conditions will damage or weaken the natural heart; some can be present without knowing it. These are some of the other conditions that can occur without knowing it that can damage or weaken the natural heart: Coronary artery and heart attack. Coronary artery disease is the most common form of heart disease and can cause heart failure.

Over time, arteries that supply blood to the heart's narrow muscle form a buildup of fatty deposits, a process called atherosclerosis. The buildup of plaques can cause reduced blood flow to our hearts. A heart attack occurs when plaques formed by fatty deposits in the arteries rupture; this causes a blood clot to form, which blocks blood flow to the area of the heart muscle. High blood pressure (hypertension): Blood pressure is the force of blood pumped by the heart through our arteries; if our blood pressure is high our heart has to work harder than it should to circulate blood throughout our bodies.

Man is an individual living in a body, having a soul and spirit. When we speak of the heart, it is the inner spirit created and hidden from the natural eye, which is the center of our emotions. These emotions are love, hate, desire, and feelings. The spiritual heart houses one's innermost thoughts and secret feelings of mankind.

The soul and mind is associated with the activity of the heart (spirit), in that the heart is the center function of the soul and thoughts in the mind. Just as the natural heart is the center functioning part of our entire body, so it is with the spiritual heart. The spiritual heart is the center functioning part of our spirit man.

If the love of God is clogged out of our spiritual hearts, in time it will cause other negative emotions to arise out of a spiritual heart, that is becomes bitter and hardened. This type of emotion will lead to hate, envy, malice, rebellion, doubt, fear, strife, unbelief, resentment, jealousy and unforgiveness. All these emotions stem from a spiritual heart that refuses to allow God's love to have total control of the spiritual heart, blocking the very presence of an intimate relationship with our creator and his fellowship and communion. It is out of the abundance of our hearts that our mouths speak. The heart is connected to our Soul, spirit and the mind; therefore the heart imagines good thoughts that are good or vain imaginable thoughts. We must think good thoughts as God gives us in accordance to Philippians 4:8 thinking on things that are honest, lovely, just, true, pure, virtuous, and of a good report if there be any praise, think on these things.

The will and emotions are closely connected to feelings and affections of a person, therefore the heart thinks, feels, decides, and desires; the heart carries out our thinking process.

This intellectual activity corresponds to what we call the mind, thus the heart understands, imagines, remembers and all decision making is carried out by our hearts. The heart is the true characteristics and personality of an individual. God knows the heart of each individual, but do you know your heart? In 1 Samuel 16:7 God says to Samuel: man looks on the outward appearance but God looks on the heart (spirit).

In our carnality or fleshly nature, we tend to focus on the outer appearance of individuals, while God the creator knows the innermost part of the spirit, soul, mind and body of each person he created. So whatever we think on or focus on the most will proceed out of our mouths that comes from the spirit, such as jealousy, hate, gossiping, backbiting, slander, faultfinding, envy, strife, unforgiveness, doubt, fear and unbelief, lying, stealing, resentment, profanity, evil thoughts, judgmental behavior, and sowing discord; all these things come from within an unpurified heart. It is important for us to know what is in our hearts, for out of the abundance of our hearts the mouth speaks; we really respond from our hearts through our mouths.

It is essential that we allow the Lord God through the word, the Holy Spirit and discernment to examine our hearts (spirit). The word of God will cleanse us of anything that is not of God. Jesus said this in the book of John in chapter 15:3 *Now you are clean through the word which I (Jesus) spoken unto you.*

We act and speak from our hearts (Proverbs 4: 23) so we must guard our hearts. In this scripture, Proverbs 4:23, we are told to *keep thy heart with all diligence for out of our hearts flows the issues of life*. Life's issues flows out of our hearts: problems with our marriages, our money, our disobedient children, homelessness, alcoholism, drug addiction, pornography, mental stress, emotional stress, uncontrolled anger, prostitution and human trafficking, and psychological problems are all issues of life.

All these issues of life stem from a root most likely proceeding out of what has affected our spiritual heart in some way.

It is vital to keep our hearts in line with the word of God, because the word of God will keep our hearts (spirit) clean. King David learns this when he sinned with Bathsheba and he penned in Psalm 51:10: *create in me a clean heart, renew in me a right spirit.* When sin is in our hearts and minds, we must quickly repent, allowing God to cleanse our hearts and renew in us a right spirit in Jesus's name, Amen. We can't have fellowship or communion with the Father and the son with an unclean spiritual heart; God will purge us if we ask him to create a clean heart within us and a right spirit in Jesus's name, Amen.

When comparing the natural heart to the spiritual heart, we need to remember our spiritual heart can get spiritual heart blockage and spiritual heart murmur, spiritual heart irregularities, spiritual prideful heart, spiritual unbelieving heart, spiritual heart attack, and spiritual heart failure, but through God's word we can recover our hearts so we will find how our hearts can be kept through the word of God. For out of the abundance of our hearts, our mouths speak, which is found in these two scriptures: *Let us know it is importance what we speak* (Matthew 12:34) and Proverbs 18:21: *When we allow God to cleanse our hearts it can be transplanted into the heart of Jesus and we will learn God's heartbeat through the power of the Holy Spirit.*

In Proverbs 18:21 we can find that there is life and death in the power of our tongues, we must watch the words that proceed out of our mouths, which comes from our hearts (spirit). Our words will cause some type of heart malfunction to our spiritual hearts if not checked through examining what is in our hearts through God's word.

In James 3:5-6, it talks about the tongue being a *little member boasting great things how great a matter a little fire it kindles. The tongue is a fire a world of iniquity so is the tongue among our members that defiles the whole body and sets on fire the very course of nature it set on the fire of hell.* Therefore, choose your words carefully by being slow to speak, quick to hear, slow to anger (James 1:19). Therefore we must lay apart all filthiness and superfluity of naughtiness and receive with meekness the engrafted word which is able to save our souls. It is important to receive the word of God with meekness to keep our heart (spirit), soul, and mind that we can remain functional as believers. When we don't stay under the microscope of the word it causes a spiritual heart to malfunction.

Just as there are different types of malfunctions in the natural heart, there are many malfunctions that take place in the spiritual heart. When the spiritual heart malfunctions we allow all types of emotions to go unchecked such as envy, bitterness, unforgiveness, strife, hate, jealousy, uncleanness of mind and heart, idolatry (Galatians 5: 20-21), worship of mankind and other things, fornication, adultery, lasciviousness, witchcraft, variance, emulation, wrath, seditions, heresies, murders, drunkenness and reveling (Matthew 12:34) .

Matthew 12:34 speaks of a *generation of vipers, how can you being evil speak good things?* For out of the abundance of your heart, the mouth speaks. Many of the above conditions will cause spiritual heart blockage, spiritual heart murmur, a spiritual hard heart that can lead to a cold, stony heart, an uncircumcised spiritual heart, spiritual heart irregularities, spiritual attack, and spiritual heart failure. As we search the scriptures, we can find a way to recover our spiritual hearts in Jesus's name, Amen.

Our heart can house wrong emotions that will hinder our spiritual heart growth such as evil, hardness of heart, rebelliousness, unforgiveness, doubt, fear, unbelief, hate, strife, and malice. All of these are wrong emotions that proceed out of our heart. If you notice there is a repeat of these negative emotions, we must continue to ask God to keep our hearts cleansed and renew us in our spirits.

Since our spiritual heart carries out our thinking process by deciding, we have been given a choice to do good or evil, blessing or curses; God will not force his will on us, the decision is to be willing to change for his good. God has given each of us a will to make right or wrong choices and make our own decisions: what will you do to keep a clean heart? The heart is connected to our minds, souls and spirits; therefore the heart imagines. The word of God has many good things we can think on such as the goodness of the Lord and his Kingdom. Amen! When we keep our minds on the Lord God, he will keep us in perfect peace (Isaiah 26:3).

It is important to bring our thoughts into the obedience of Jesus Christ, casting down vain imagination and the things that would exalt itself against the knowledge of God. The Apostle Paul speaks of this in 2 Corinthians 10:4-6 (amplified version): *for the weapons of our warfare aren't physical weapons of the flesh and blood but they are mighty before God for the overthrow and destruction of strongholds.*

Insomuch as we refute arguments, theories, and reasoning and every proud and lofty thing that sets itself up against the true knowledge of God and we lead every thought and purpose away captive into the obedience of Christ the anointed one, being in readiness to punish every insubordinate for his disobedience, when your own submission and obedience are fully secured and complete. (Amplified version) We cannot reason with God about his plan and destinies for our lives; we must be committed, yielded, and obedient to his will and purpose.

This is the very reason we must know how the heart and mind connects because as a person thinks, so will he become. Proverbs 23:7 says *for as he thinks in his heart so is he, eat and drink, say he to thee but his heart isn't with thee.* If we continue to say these words: am broke, lack, poverty, sickness, disease, hate, envy, jealousy, bitterness, unforgiving, we speak these things and they will become a reality. Caught up into the way of the destroyer of our spiritual life, the devil who comes to steal, kill, and destroy. When Satan is the killer, stealer and the destroyer, we must know our authority against this destructive enemy of our spiritual heart will come; we must stay alert and aware of him and his demonic army.

(Luke 10:19) We have been given power and authority over all the powers of the wicked one and nothing shall by any means hurt us; speaking only the word of God that is activated, alive, quick and powerful as we speak it out of our mouths; believing it in our hearts it shall come to pass in Jesus's name, hallelujah.

As we have been given power and authority over our enemy, it is important to know the keys we have is of the

Kingdom of God; these keys represent authority to use against the kingdom of darkness. We must have a relationship with God and know who he is and who he has called us to be in his Kingdom, not a religious mindset as the Pharisees and Sadducees. It is very important to know the word of God and how to use it, for God's word is alive and powerful.

We must keep our thoughts in captivity with Christ Jesus by being renewed in the spirit of our minds daily through the Living Word of God. (Ephesians 4:23) In this scripture we read: *to be renewed in the spirit of our mind.* Therefore, the heart and mind connected must be kept pure and clean thoughts through the living word of God.

When we speak of the heart, it is translated spirit. Remember, God is a spirit and we are regenerated spirits with a new heart transformed into the heartbeat of God. In Romans 10:9-10 it says we confess with our mouth and believe in our heart that Jesus is the son of God, therefore the heart and mouth connects. How important our spiritual heart is to our salvation, believing in our hearts (spirit) and confessing with our mouths that Jesus came at the command of his Father; for God so loved the world he gave Jesus that we through him may obtain eternal life.

We must know the heartbeat of God by abiding in his word, which is spirit and life. The word of God is alive; according to Hebrews 4:12 amplified version, it says the word God speaks, is alive and full of power making it active, operative, energizing, and effective, it is sharper than any two-edged sword, penetrating to the dividing line of the breath of life, soul, and immortal spirit and of the joints and marrow of the deepest parts of our nature, exposing, sifting, analyzing and judging the very thoughts and purpose of the heart (spirit). Therefore the word of God brings his life (Spirit) into our spirit, causing the power of life to be activated, to be operative by energizing, making us effective, through the sharpened two-edged sword (God's word) to penetrate the dividing line of the very breath of life and soul, the immortal spirit by joints and marrow of the deepest parts of the heart (spirit). The changes of our hearts comes through this life-changing operative, penetrating, energizing effective God-breathed refreshing wind to empower our hearts (spirit). The refreshing wind is the same wind that was present on the day the Pentecost as the Holy Spirit came as a mighty rushing wind.

We must allow the Holy Spirit and the word of God to examine our spiritual hearts. Just as we go to our natural physician, we must stay under the microscopic word of God and the authority of the Greatest Physician Jesus Christ, who specializes in things that are impossible and nothing shall be impossible when we believe.

When we get the word of God into our heart as it is written, it will be activated, be operative, energizing to our spirit, soul, and mind. It will help us by penetrating the very core of our spirit to the dividing line of our breath of life, our immortal spirit to the very joints and marrow of the deepest part of our spirits. This living word will transform us daily as we abide in this word of God.

As the word is spirit, light and life, it will enlighten our spirit, soul and mind allowing the word to purify our hearts, soul and mind, cleansing and washing our spirit to be transformed into the image and likeness of Jesus Christ. God deals with our hearts. Jesus spoke of us allowing him to enter in our hearts. As he knocks on the doors of our hearts, we must be willing to let Jesus come into our hearts, for he will not force his way in. This is found in the book of Revelation 3:20 which reads: B*ehold I (Jesus) stand the door and knock; if any man hear my voice and open the door I will come in to him, sup with him and he with me.* The door that Jesus was knocking on is the door to our hearts; we need to allow him to examine our spirit (heart), soul, and mind and let him in to revive and restore you back to his divine life. He should be the first lover of our lives.

Jesus knocks at the doors of our hearts, but we must hear his voice, then we must obey his voice. As we hear and obey Jesus's voice and let him in, he will come into our hearts, and our lives will never be the same. Jesus calls us into his Kingdom because the Father doesn't want anyone to perish. We must be willing for him to break up the hardness of our hearts. As we open up to the spirit of God by accepting Jesus as our savior and Lord, we go through a lifetime of change and growing up in the grace and knowledge of who he is.

When we let Jesus into our hearts (spirits) we gain the heartbeat of God, and the Father and the son will come in to make their abode with us, and they will fellowship and communion with us in the spirit.

As we yield our hearts (spirits) to God and his son, we learn to follow the leading of the Holy Spirit. God will reveal himself to us. An intimate relationship will give us a refreshing wind of the breath of God, refreshing our spirits, souls, minds and body in Jesus's name, Amen.

We must realize without our God, our flesh and heart will fail us, but God will strengthen our hearts and our portion forever according to Psalm 73:26.

As we learn to give our spirits (hearts) over to the Lord God through the word, praise and worship, our lives will take on new meaning and we will never be the same; we become the image of the one that can transform our entire being. Amen.

Chapter Two

BIBLICAL MEDICAL POCEDURES FOR HEALING AND GOD'S WORD FOR HEALING

Learning Biblical Medical Procedures to Healing Natural Diseases

In the study of Eastern literature, we find numerous references to physicians and medical practices. In Mesopotamia about 2700 B.C. a Sumerian physician named Lulu lived in this city. There was an Egyptian named Imhotep who established a reputation as a physician and priest.

Imhotep was a noted architect who designed the step pyramid at Saqqara. They had a code of Hammurabi from 1750 B.C. that contains laws regulating the practice of medicine in its infancy; the many practitioners slowly improved their skills.

The Egyptians made more rapid progress in medical knowledge and its application to patients than the Babylonians. The Babylonian physicians tended to specialize in one part of the body, such as the eye, the teeth, or the stomach. The Egyptian physicians often used herbs in their medications. The Egyptian physicians became respected throughout the ancient world; their skills were admired in later periods by the Greeks, who eventually became the foremost physicians. Egyptians were called to embalm the body of Jacob (Genesis 50:2). King Asa sought medical care from Hippocrates. The Greeks established an important medical school in Alexandra, Egypt, which flourished for several centuries and trained many physicians. The school was noted for its large library and laboratory facilities.

The Romans made significant contributions in the area of public health, including the provisions for pure water supply, effectiveness of a sewage disposal system, and establishment of food inspection programs. The Romans also established network hospitals, which initially founded the care for the needs of the army. In many lands, priests were assigned to medical duties; this was among the ancient

Hebrews, where priests were the major providers of medical services. The priests were responsible for the diagnosis of diseases that were a threat to the community (Lev. 13).

Priests in Israel apparently played a very little role in the actual treatment of the ill persons. During the time of the New Testament, the Roman god of healing, Aesculapius (known by the Greeks in earlier times by the name of Asclepius), who was popular among them, the person seeking to be healed would throng the temple, often bringing small replicas of the portion of the body that was afflicted by the disease.

THE WORD of GOD'S HEALING POWER

God's word heals Physical and Spiritual Diseases through Faith and belief

The Bible contains little information about the treatment of diseases, except miraculous means such the pool of Bethesda (John 5:1-15), the pool of Siloam connected with Jesus's ministry of healing (John 9:7), and the woman with the issue of blood (Matthew 5:25 -30). Medical care in Biblical times frequently employed the use of different kinds of salve and ointments; olive oil was widely used alone or as an ingredient in ointments for treating wounds (Isaiah 1:6, Luke 10:34). Oil was a symbol of medicine coupled with prayer for the ill (Mark 6:13, James 5:14).

Herbs and various products obtained from different plants was among the ancient medicines; these were applied to the body as poultices or in many cases taken by mouth. Frankincense and myrrh, gum resins obtained from trees, were commonly used in perfumes and incense; wine was also used to soothe the stomach and intestinal disorders, and beer was used as an ingredient in several medications.

Since there was relatively little good medical care available, illnesses often led to disastrous results. The sick in Biblical times divined help through faith and prayer. Today with research, doctors' help, and the study of the human body through educational means, those who study the heart as specialists such as Cardiology, their specialty is matters of our human heart. In our spiritual hearts there is only one who specializes in matters of our spiritual hearts, and all that concerns the soul, mind, spirit and body that is Jesus, who knows the heart of each of us.

In 2 Chronicles 6:30, it says: *then hear thou from heaven thy dwelling place and forgive and render to every man according unto his ways, whose heart thou knows; for thou only knows the hearts of the children of men.* This is why we must know the difference between the natural and spiritual hearts; the spiritual side of the heart can affect us in the physical realm, and what affects us in the spirit realm will sometimes affect us in the natural realm. It is important that we guard our hearts diligently at all times. Just as in the medical profession the study of the human heart has a specialist known as a Cardiologist and who specializes in all things concerning the heart.

We must allow Jesus to keep our spiritual hearts healthy by studying the word on everything concerning our spiritual heart, which is a huge task. There are many types of heart diseases or malfunctions that can occur in the spiritual heart. We must study what disease is in our spiritual heart and how it affects us spiritually and naturally.

As we have discussed in this chapter, the natural procedures of healing the natural heart, we have also discussed the spiritual procedures of healing our spiritual hearts. Jesus is the healing balm for the entire heart, body, soul, mind and spirit. Psalm 103:1-6 says: *Bless the Lord O my soul and all that is within me, bless his holy name, bless the Lord O my soul, and forget not all his benefits, who forgive all thine iniquities, who heals all thy diseases, who redeems thy life from destruction, who crowns thee with loving kindness and tender mercies, who satisfies thy mouth with good things so that thy youth is renewed like and eagle. The Lord executes righteousness and judgment for all that are oppressed.*

Now, as our discussion goes further into what is the meaning of a disease, and how a disease can be physical, emotional, relational, spiritual and psychological and physiological, these conditions can limit our human functioning, lessening the quality of life if left unchecked.

Chapter Three

THE MEANING OF DISEASE IN THE NATURAL AND SPIRITUAL HEART

What is the meaning of Dis-ease?

A disease can be physical, emotional, psychological, relational and spiritual; all these conditions can limit human functioning and lessen the quality of life if left unchecked. A successful treatment of a disease depends upon a primary prompt, correct diagnosis and prognosis of our spiritual hearts by the use of effective therapeutic, microscopic agents of the word of God and the Holy Spirit. What do we find in this word, "disease?" "Dis" means to pull apart different parts of the body, away from organs and systems. The word "ease" means to relieve, to smooth, bring relaxation, freedom from shame or trouble, to make one comfortable, to loosen, to be at rest, to bring contentment. Example: We confess what is in our hearts to the Lord, and God will bring comfort to our spirits. God knows how to smooth every pain, every hurt, free us from trouble, comfort us and give us rest from heartaches in Jesus's name, Amen.

What does the word disease mean in reference to a spiritual heart? First of all, the word itself means to pull apart, to lack, to draw away from, a condition, organs, systems or parts doesn't function properly.

Therefore, disease in a spiritual heart will cause the members to pull apart, draw away, cause the system of the Kingdom of God to malfunction and cause disunity and discord among the members of the body of Jesus.

These also are issues that proceed from the heart, which will cause spiritual heart trouble in the members of the body of Christ. These issues can and will lead to spiritual heart disease such as having an unpure spiritual heart, spiritual deceptive heart, spiritual prideful heart, spiritual uncircumcised heart, spiritual heart blockage, spiritual hard heart, and/or spiritual heart attack. Spiritual heart transplant must occur before healing can take place from spiritual heart failure. We must take these issues to the secret place with the great Physician Jesus so that healing can take place. The word of God is just like the scalpel of a surgeon that cuts away any scar tissue in our spiritual hearts.

We will have to have spiritual heart surgery to get rid of any of these heart diseases through the sword of the spirit which is the word of God; the attending physician's instrument for healing is the living word. This is called circumcising our spiritual heart of all that will cause us not to grow up spiritually and mature. We must keep alert to know that none of these diseases keep us pulled apart, draw us away from our Kingdom assignments, stop the system of the Kingdom from working, be so organized that the focus of the Kingdom is denied by our hidden and own agendas causing malfunctioning of God's ordained Kingdom work.

We are many members functioning by the power of the Holy Spirit only to work the work of God's Kingdom, calling heaven down to the earth's realm in Jesus's name. As many members in the body of Jesus Christ, we have been given different gifts of the spirit to work in harmony with the Holy Spirit and one another. In 1 Corinthians 12:1-14 it says:

Verse 1: *Now concerning spiritual gifts, brethren, I would not have you ignorant.*

Verse 2: *You know that you were Gentiles carried away unto these dumb idols, even as you were led.*

Verse 3: *Wherefore I give you to understand, that no man speaking by the Spirit of God call Jesus accursed: and that no man can say that Jesus is the Lord, but by the Holy Ghost.*

Verse 4: *Now there are diversities of gifts, but the same Spirit.*

Verse 5: *And there are differences of administrations, but the same Lord.*

Verse 6: *And there are diversities of operations, but it is the same God which works all in all.*

Verse 7: *But manifestation of the Spirit is given to every man to profit withal.*

Verse 8: *For to one is given by the Spirit the word of wisdom; to another the word of knowledge by the same Spirit.*

Verse 9: *To another faith by the same Spirit; to another the gifts of healing by the same Spirit.*

Verse 10: *To another the working of miracles, to another prophecy, to another discerning of spirits, to another divers kinds of tongues, to another the interpretation of tongues.*

Verse 11: *But all these work that one and the self-same Spirit, dividing to every man severally as he will.*

Verse 12: *For as the body is one, and hath many members, and all the members of that one body, being many, are one body so also is Christ.*

Verse 13: *For by one Spirit are we all baptized into one body, whether we be Jew or Gentles, whether we be bond or free, and have been all made to drink into one Spirit.*

Verse 14: *For the body is not one member but many.*

Since we have all been baptized into the body of Jesus Christ, we can't be separated by our differences of gifts; these gifts are given to work in the Kingdom of God for his purposes and plan of the Kingdom. There is only one big eye and that is Jesus and the great (I am) God the Father. It is not our titles and positions that make us Kingdom ambassadors; it is having Jesus as the center focus in our lives and being sold out for the King.

In lining up with the will of God's word, we have to have a made-up mind for his service and count up the cost for living a crucified lifestyle of denial. There is a great price to pay for God's anointing because it is God's anointing and he anoints each one of us for his service. Some of us take this anointing as if it personally belongs to us; it is God's and when we touch God's anointing we are touching him, that is why it is dangerous to touch God's anointed vessels because we are touching God; not the individual person, but God himself.

We must search our hearts by aligning our will to the will of God, which is his word. Abiding in God's word allows us to abide in Jesus. (John 14:4-7) *Abide in me and I in you, as the branch cannot bear fruit of itself except it abide in the vine no more except you abide in me.* When we will not allow the word of God to examine our diseased spiritual heart, the spiritual heart begins to harden. We cannot bring forth the fruit of the Kingdom of God without abiding in the true vine (Jesus). We must not be in denial of any spiritual heart diseases in order to be restored back to a spiritual healthy heart.

We will deal with each of these spiritual heart issues by the attending physician, Jesus; he will make a diagnosis and prognosis of each affected area of our spiritual hearts. The Holy Spirit will be assisting Jesus in the treatment of our spiritual hearts, for he is searching and knows the inner secrets of our spiritual hearts.

We first will define the meaning of the word *diagnosis*; a diagnosis is an act or process of identifying a disease by carefully investigating the symptoms. In order to reach the healing process of the conditions of our spiritual hearts, we must have a plan for the cure; this is called *prognosis* which means identifying the probable cause of a disease and how to treat a disease resulting in the treatment.

God's word works through instruments and ways he chooses to bring health to sick people, spiritually, emotionally and physically. The emphasis on healing was particularly in Jesus's ministry and in the early church; nearly one-fifth of the Gospels report Jesus's miracles. The Gospels record fourteen distinct instances of physical and mental healing. Jesus commissioned his disciples to continue his basic ministry including healing (Matthew 10:5-10: Mark 6:7-13). In the book of Acts the healing ministry continued. This message of healing is for today's disciples to continue the basic ministry of Jesus as he has commissioned us, for God is the same yesterday, today and forever. In the statement below we can see how the word *psychosomatic* identifies the relation of body and spirit being inseparable.

Psychosomatic is a word which literally means soul and body, referring to the close relationship of body and spirit. The soul affects the body, and health of the soul may be an indication of the health of the body. John wanted for his friend Gaius to prosper in every way and be in good health (3 John 2). This was an anticipation of the emphasis of psychosomatic medicine: a person is a unit; body and soul cannot be separated.

Most Christians believe in healing through faith, but trying to decide what techniques are scriptural, decorous, and psychologically helpful confuses the believer; Jesus used different methods in his healing ministry. They included calling upon the individuals' faith, touching the sick person or bystanders to be healed, praying, assuring forgiveness of sin, uttering commands, and using physical means.

These are Biblical teachings that Jesus taught:

(1) The Bible clearly states Jesus believed in healing of the body.

(2) Jesus spoke of doctors in a positive way as he compared those in good health who have no need of a physician with those who do (Matthew 9:12; Mark 2:17; Luke 5:31). God has often healed by the way he has led scientists into discovery of body function.

(3) The methods of healing Jesus used included prayer, laying on of hands, anointing with oil and assurance of forgiveness of sins; the church continues to use these methods (James 5:14-16).

(4) Jesus did not use healing as a means of gaining attention but tried to keep the experience private. Praise the Lord. He heals all our diseases (Psalm 103: 2-3).

We will be examining the conditions of our spiritual hearts by identifying the symptoms of what has affected the different parts of our spiritual hearts to reach a diagnosis, the probable cause of treating the diseased area, and the result of the treatment through the healing of the word of God and leading of the Holy Spirit for prescriptions.

As we examine our hearts by taking an inventory of our hearts in unforgiveness, hurts, wounds of the past, any wrong motives, and bad attitudes, the Holy Spirit will reveal to us what needs to be dealt with; but we have to be honest with ourselves in order to get treatment from the attending physician Jesus Christ, and the Holy Spirit will write the corrective prescriptions needed. The secret to our healing is repentance, prayer and fasting; some things will only come through fasting and praying (Matthew 17: 21) *howbeit these kind go out, but by prayer and fasting*. We must not allow our spiritual heart arteries to clog up with any uncleanness of envy, hate, malice, strife, bitterness, jealousy, or holding grudges and even resentment; it will stop the flow of the Holy Spirit moving in our lives. God sent Jesus to make and set us free indeed. Amen

We must give the Lord God our whole heart and draw not back to the ways and cares of the world. Don't be deceived. God will not be marked; whatever we sow, good or bad, we will receive; so in order to get completely healed we must release any unhealthy attributes not pleasing to Father God, in the name of Jesus.

Below is a prayer to help us ask our heavenly Father to examine our hearts through the power of his word and the Holy Ghost:

Father God, we come to you asking you to help us to allow you to effectively examine all parts of our spiritual heart conditions that we might be all that you have created us to be in your Kingdom. We need you in every situation, circumstance and problem that we may face through our Christian journey, things that come to trouble our hearts and minds, strengthen us in our weaknesses and build us up in your love, joy, peace, wisdom, knowledge and understanding of who you are and who you created us to be in you in faith, trust and belief; help us to watch and pray, create in us clean hearts and right spirits through your word. Keep transforming us into the image of your son Jesus, in his name we pray. Amen. God has the answer for us in all our trouble and by the name of the God of Abraham, Isaac and Jacob; God will sit us up on high and defend us (Psalm 20:1).

Chapter Four

EXAMINING THE SPIRITUAL HEART

Examination of the Spiritual Heart

The successful diagnosis and treatment of our spiritual heart is made through the power of the word of God and the guidance of the Holy Spirit, that can give us a prompt and correct treatment plan by using an effective therapeutic microscopic agent of the living word of God by putting our hearts under the examination of the microscopic word that is life and spirit. Hebrews 4:12 Amplified version says: *For the word that God speaks is alive and full of power (making it active, operative, energizing and effective); it is sharper than any two-edged sword penetrating to the dividing line of the breath of life (soul) and the immortal spirit and joints and marrow of the deepest parts of our nature) exposing and sifting and analyzing, judging the very thoughts and purpose of the heart.*

In examining our spiritual heart, the word that God speaks is alive for us and full of power that makes it active as we speak it in the atmosphere, it is operative and energizing our lives to be effective to every area of our spiritual heart and spiritual life that will affect our natural lives as well. The word is sharper than any two-edged sword that penetrates to the dividing line of our God-given spiritual breath of life (soul); the immoral spirit, joints, and marrow of our deepest parts of our nature, exposing, analyzing, and judging the very thoughts of our spiritual hearts.

Therefore the word of God will cut away the very foreskin of sin and anything that doesn't represent the life of Jesus Christ. The word of God is sharper than any surgeon's scalpel and any razor's blade cutting to the very breath of life to the deepest part of our nature; exposing, shifting, analyzing and judging the core of our spiritual hearts. It takes coming into the realities of allowing the Holy Spirit and the word working together and yielding to God in our spirits as we come into thanksgiving, praise and worship; God will reveal our hearts to us in his very presence. Let's look at coming before God's presence as we are directed by the Holy Spirit.

We are coming into the presence of the Great Physician Jesus who wants to give us our annual spiritual heart check-up; now we have made an appointment in prayer to communicate and talk to the Father about some heart irregularities. The Holy Spirit has been talking about our spiritual attitude, showing us there is a root cause to our attitude, staying away from fellowship with the brothers and sisters of our churches, complaining about the preacher preaches too long, having more of a faultfinding spirit here lately, gossiping about other members in the church and telling a few white lies, coming to church but really in a backslidden state of mind, coming into Sunday School and Church later and later, never in intercessory or spending private time alone with God and the word of God anymore, making a lot of excuses now and then.

Always saying something like "What is wrong with Sister Cookie?" and "They look at me funny." Thinking wrong thoughts of others because the beam is in our own eyes have blinded us. Have we really examined what's going on in our spiritual hearts before we pass judgment on someone else?

Let's take some type of inventory of our spiritual hearts, realizing the problem is in us. In 2 Chronicles 6:29 we read that *the prayer or supplication what so ever shall be made of any man or of all thy people Israel, when everyone shall know his own sore and his own grief and shall spread forth his hands in this house.* We may be in denial of a spiritual heart condition going on in our lives; the pressures of getting angry quickly, the few lies we tell, the meanness to others, the rudeness, the resentments of others, the faultfinding, the complaining, the backbiting, the disrespect of a person, the grumbling, the worship of material things; these issues have caused a sore in our spirits and these roots must be severed. We need to repent and turn away from these wicked ways by seeking the face of God and not his hand. As we continue to look at 2 Chronicles 6:29-30 and 2 Chronicles 7:14, we will find there is a sore in our spiritual hearts that needs healing, and learn we must turn from our wicked ways and pray that God may heal our land.

Then hear thou from heaven thy dwelling place and forgive and render unto every man according unto all his ways whose heart thou know for only thou know the hearts of the children of men. ~ 2 Chronicles 6:30

There is nothing hidden from God; he sees and knows all things. Man looks on the outer appearance; God knows our beginning to the very end of our life span. We must trust God in everything that pertains to our hearts (spirit). God knows us better than we know ourselves; it is foolish to think we are smarter than the one that created us. 2 Chronicles 7:14 says *if my people who are called by my name would humble themselves and pray turn from their wicked ways then will I hear from heaven and heal their land.* It is past time to turn from our wickedness and reacquaint ourselves with the Lord God and fall in love with him all over again.

As we allow the word and the Holy Spirit to access our spiritual heart and take a spiritual EKG called DEEP (meaning Dividing Energizing Effective Penetrating), examination of our very thoughts and immortal breath of our very nature of our hearts. When the word and Holy Spirit examine our hearts it will expose any malfunction it discovers, but we must acknowledge these irregularities quickly in order for healing to take place.

In the examination of my own spiritual heart through the power of the Holy Spirit and the word of God, I found my heart had been wounded from church hurt, some unforgiveness, betrayal by those who pretended to be my sisters or brothers in Christ Jesus who wore a mask, financial losses, losing a home to wrong mortgage lenders, losing jobs and some cars, people that were deceptive, false accusers, being lied on; my heart was so broken, but I had to realize it was all a part of the plan of God to see if I trusted him and wouldn't doubt but only believe. The medicine of the prescription of God's word worked some spiritual miracles, my faith to overcome obstacles that Jesus helped me through, and he is still helping through.

It was through turning my plate over, seeking the face and Kingdom of God with all my heart, soul, and mind, bringing every thought into the will and obedience of Jesus Christ, getting in the birth position to birth forth God's destiny for my life. Yes, I said getting in the birth position to birth forth my destiny; Satan don't want God's destiny to come forth in any of our lives, so you have to push your destiny out through getting in the position of intense intercessory prayer, being committed, to surrender all, to be sold out to God and becoming a yielded vessel of honor; praying until your spiritual bags of water break (called breakthrough), seeking the perfect will of God with every fiber of the deepest core of your soul. This is called denying yourself by being sold out completely to the plan, purpose, and destiny God has for your life; it takes perseverance, pressing into the very secret place of the Most High God, entering in the Holy of Holies, putting on the robe of righteousness, and only God can cloth us with his son Jesus which is transforming us into the very image of Jesus. God can only see us through the Blood of Jesus and he sees us as Jesus is in him and we are in the Spirit of him, we become one with them. Even in the book of Galatians 4:19 the Apostle Paul spoke of *travailing in birth until Christ be formed in them*. Read this book and verse, receive the revelation from the Holy Spirit. Jesus is being formed in us through the word, which is Jesus that became flesh, and dwelt among us. Now Jesus is in us. When Jesus is formed in us it is called transformation into his image and this is how our God sees us transformed into the image of Christ Jesus, Amen.

As I allowed the anointing of the Holy Spirit to destroy every yoke of the hindrances of my enemies and every assigned demon that came to steal, kill, and destroy God's destiny for my life has changed me. Every yoke is broken and destroyed. Every chain is destroyed in the mighty name of JESUS; the chains are still being broken. The more you and I surrender all to Jesus the more we become as Jesus is in the Father, Amen. We have been positioned in heavenly places to sit with Jesus far above principalities, powers, and dominions. It is past time to take our rightful places in the Body of Jesus Christ. This is why when we go through our spiritual heart examination, we need to receive the diagnosis and get the correct prognosis for our spiritual heart prescriptions and get our healing.

As all of us will go through some type of spiritual heart conditions during our spiritual journeys, we must get into the birth position to birth forth our destinies too. Isaiah 66:7-14 says this:

Verse 7: *Before she travailed, she brought forth: before her pain came, she was delivered of a man child.*

Verse 8: *Who hath heard such a thing? Who hath seen such things? Shall the earth be made to bring forth in one day? Or shall a nation be born at once? For as soon as Zion travailed, she brought forth children.*

Verse 9: *Shall I (The Lord God) bring to the birth and not cause to bring forth? Said the Lord: shall I cause to bring forth and shut up the womb? God said it. God will cause us to get in the birth position and give birth to our destinies and we have to push it forth in the secret place of intercessory prayer.*

Verse 10: *Rejoice you with Jerusalem and be glad with her. All you that love her: rejoice for joy with her, all that mourn for her. Mourning is a type of travailing, as a woman is in pain before she is delivered of the baby in child birth.*

Verse 11: *That you may suck and be satisfied with the breasts of her consolations: that you may milk out and be delighted with the abundance of her glory. God is our consolidator as we drink of the Living well water of his Spirit we will be satisfied and filled.*

Verse 12: *For thus said the Lord, behold I will extend peace to her like a river, and the glory of the gentiles like a flowing stream. Then shall you suck, you shall be born upon her sides and be dandled upon her knees.*

Verse 13: *As one whom his mother comforted, so will I (God) comfort you: and you shall be comforted in Jerusalem. God will comfort his people and he sent Jesus to take our place on the cross and raise him up again to restore us back to his spiritual life; and Jesus sent the Comforter, the intercessor, the advocate, the strengthener, the Helper, the Standby in the person of The Holy Spirit.*

Verse 14: *And when you see this your heart shall rejoice and your bones shall flourish like an herb and the hand of the Lord shall be known toward his servants, and his indignation toward his enemies.*

We don't have to fret because of the enemies of our souls. God is our shield and protector, Amen. This is why if you give everything in our hearts to God in intercessory prayer, by casting all our cares upon God he will take care of it all.

Peter 5:7 Amplified Version says: *Casting the whole of your care all your anxieties, all your worries, all your concerns, once and for all on Him (God) He cares for you watchfully.*

God's word purified my heart, mind, soul, and spirit. The refreshing wind of the Holy Spirit restored my joy, my peace with God, and my love for him and his people. Now I know what Jesus meant when he said Father forgive them for they know not what they do.

God gave me the Scriptural medicine of his living word to revive me, replenish me, and restore me to the abundant life of his son Jesus. I am in total freedom, washed by the word and the sanctifying blood of Jesus Christ. God wants to give each of us Scriptural medicine to bringing restoration, revival, replenish us in every spiritual heart valve, to unclog, unblock any part of our spiritual hearts that have been affected in any way by spiritual hurt, wounds, pains or any misunderstanding of spiritual heart trouble.

We all go through heartaches but we must not deny or deceive ourselves if we want healing to take place. The devil will put all kinds of distractions and deceptions in our lives; we must be alert and watchful at all times and praying for a greater discernment.

I had to remember that no weapons formed against me would prosper; but God's word says no weapon formed against us can prosper and every tongue that would rise up against me I can condemn (Isaiah 54:17). I had to remember to keep a heart of repentance to forgive and let it go in order to get answers to my prayers and the blessings to flow out of my heart of obedience to the word of God; being willing and obedient that I may eat the good of the land in Jesus's name, according to Isaiah 1:19.

Many people came appearing to be of God but were sent by the deceiver and because of God's discerning spirit, I recognized the spirit behind the person; the evil plots, the schemes, the tricks, the evil slanderers, the discord sowers. Above all, to recognize the spirit of pride to keep it under my feet, the devices of the kingdom of darkness must stay bound up in Jesus's name Amen. You will be able to recognize these same spirits of darkness too, by keeping a clean heart, a right spirit, by the leading of the Holy Spirit. It is very important for the children of God to stand fast in the liberty in which Jesus Christ has set us free, and we allow our hearts to be examined by and through the word daily. Our hearts can remain clean by being sensitive to the Holy Spirit. The more God blesses us with his knowledge of being strong in Christ Jesus we need to remain humble under his Mighty hand. Amen.

This is our prognosis Prayer: Our Father in heaven we come to you in the mighty name of Jesus that you give us a greater discernment of your Spirit to help us know the devices of the kingdom of darkness.

God has given us his word to use against the kingdom of darkness as we remind the demons and their lord of the power of the word which is Jesus and His precious blood that is very powerful to us. So Father God we stand in faith believing the authority that Jesus has given us in his mighty name. According to Luke 10:19, we take the authority of having all power over all the power of the enemy and nothing shall by any means hurt us. Father God, we thank you for seating us in heavenly places with Christ Jesus far above principalities, powers, rulers of the darkness of this world and spiritual wickedness in high places; we take our stand in Jesus's name, Amen.

Chapter Five

SPIRITUAL HEART MALFUNCTION

What happens when the Spiritual Heart Malfunctions?

At one point in our Christian journey we will all experience some type of spiritual heart malfunction. What causes a spiritual heart to malfunction? Let me explain. In the natural life we all have issues that proceed from the hidden things in our hearts and minds. It can stem from our emotions, relationships, marriages, abuse verbally or mentally, a psychological disorder, or a physiological disorder, even a sociological disorder; all must be dealt with one way or the other.

At times, life issues can be overwhelming, causing stress, sleeplessness, a troubling chain of thoughts, financial situations, doubt, fear of losing a job, fear of homelessness, growing old, sickness, diseases, marriage problems, divorce, support to our children, unruly children, problems in school, to name a few. It takes finding the right verse and chapter of the word of God to overcome such. As Psalm 142:1-3 says: *I cried unto the Lord with my voice: with my voice unto the Lord did I make my supplication. I poured out my complaint before him: I showed before him my trouble. When my spirit was overwhelmed within me, then thou knew my path. In the way wherein I walked they privily laid a snare for me.*

These various situations and circumstances can be so overwhelming until it can affect our minds and some part of our spiritual hearts. Many of these problems must be dealt with through finding the root of the problems; there is always an underlying root to what one might go through. Remember it all starts in our spirit (heart) and comes out of our mouths; when we are hurting financially it may come out in anger or shouting profanity. The cause of the problem is the lack of money that is the root to hurting in our bank account, lack of hours worked, layoff, not balancing our budgets; these are a few examples of what I mean by the root cause to a problem. These and other malfunctions can occur in the spiritual heart; they are uncleanness, idolatry, adultery, fornication, lasciviousness, witchcraft, variance, emulation, envying, wrath, malice, hate, unforgiveness, seditions, heresies, murders, and drunkenness. These are called works of the flesh according to Galatians 5:19-21.

Matthew 6:21 speaks about the treasure of the heart. Wherever our treasures are, that is where our hearts will be. What do we sometimes treasure in our hearts? Our homes, our cars, our clothes, our husbands and wives, children, education, degrees and titles; we must know the difference in what we let fill our hearts more than God. This is always a heart malfunction, when we put things before the giver of every good and perfect gift. We must open up our hearts to the one and only creator of the heaven and this earth; he desires to give us good things, but we must put him first, and his Kingdom and all his righteousness.

There are all types of solutions to helping a malfunctioning spiritual heart. If you are stressed, find ways to relieve the stress through an exercise program; seek a financial advisor if you don't have good budgeting skills; seek a marriage counselor if you are having marriage problem; if you are divorced, seek out other divorcees befriending them to see what you have in common; for unruly children, seek counseling, it could be because of the absent parent. Solutions you might consider along with getting into the word for spiritual refreshing of your spirit man. Our hearts can really be transformed through the word and prayer if we believe, trust, and obey the word.

As we allow the Holy Spirit to examine our spiritual hearts, focus on what he will reveal to us, during our quiet time of prayer and meditation; the Holy Spirit will speak to our spirit man as to how to restore any area of our spiritual heart that we might be healed.

Always wait upon the Lord and be encouraged (Psalm 27:1-14). The joy of knowing the Lord will heal a diseased heart, and will be a continued strength to us. Nehemiah 8:10: *The joy of the Lord is my strength.* God wants us to be strengthened in our spiritual heart. Let him do the work now and we yield ourselves to the leading of his spirit. Amen.

There are many scriptural references to keep joy in our hearts through the word of God; we will have to find and locate the word that describes spiritual situations. Study them, believe them, and acknowledge them to change any spiritual heart conditions.

One prescription after examining our hearts is found in Joshua 1:6-9. *Be strong and of a good courage for unto this people shall thou divide for an inheritance the land, which I (God) swear unto their fathers to give them. Only be thou strong and very courageous that thou may observe to do according to all the law, which Moses my servant commanded thee: turn not from the right hand or to the left, that thou may prosper withers ever thou go. This book of the law shall not depart out of thy mouth, but thou shall meditate therein day and night, that thou may observe to do according to all that is written therein, for then thou shall make thy way prosperous and then thou shalt have good success. Have I not commanded thee? Be strong and of a good courage, be not afraid neither be thou dismayed for the Lord thy God is with thee wither ever thou go.*

Therefore when our spiritual hearts malfunction there is always a solution found in God's word; the key to any malfunctioned heart is to search the scriptures like Joshua 1:6-9. This chapter and verses has many gold nuggets to strengthen us in our spiritual heart malfunctions. Let's find a nugget. *Remember the word is a lamp unto our feet and a light unto our path* (Psalm 119:105). The words in Joshua allows us to see how meditating in God's word will keep us strong and courageous as we observe it as it is written; meditating on the word of God gives us his success plan that we can be prosperous wherever we go. If we observe and do the word, prosperity and good success will enter into our lives and God will be with us wherever we go.

Prayer: Heavenly Father we come to you asking you to help us to bring any spiritual malfunctioning heart to you. Because you look on to our hearts we ask you to search our hearts and reveal to us anything that isn't pleasing to you. We need clean hearts to serve and obey you and to be pleasing in your sight, to help us to remain forgiving, loving, gentle, kind and understanding. Keep us under the spirit of God, humble, allowing the therapeutic microscopic word to sift, penetrate, energize, dividing between our nature and spirit, for the word and Holy Spirit knows the intent of our hearts. We surrender, yield, give ourselves totally to the third person of the trinity to teach, lead us, and guide us into all your truth in Jesus's name, Amen.

These are the very scriptures it took to get my spiritual heart in alignment with God's word, meditating day and night to get my heart healthy again. It didn't happen overnight, but I had to keep working at it because it is a continuous heart exercise to keep our spiritual heart in alignment with the heartbeat of God through studying and staying in the word daily and communication through prayer. Alignment is the key to coming to God's perfect order in our spiritual hearts.

Chapter Six

THE DIAGOSING AND PROGNOSING OF A SPIRITUAL HEART

How to Diagnose and give a Prognosis to the Spiritual Heart

We have to study our spiritual heart to allow the attending physician Jesus to make a diagnosis of our spiritual heart trouble; it is through our appointment in prayer of intense intercession that the Holy Spirit will reveal what type of spiritual malfunctions have occurred during our spiritual journey. This is when we must take some spiritual inventory of what the Holy Spirit has revealed to us.

An Unforgiving Spiritual Heart is found in the example below: In some other pages we will give a complete diagnosis and prognosis of this spiritual heart malfunction.

Example: The Holy Spirit has found we have some unforgiveness in a part of our spiritual heart that is affecting how we speak to the others who may not have hurt us or mistreated us, but we take it out on them because someone else did us wrong. We keep justifying how they did us wrong, but the Holy Spirit says "Let it go; forgive." We keep holding on until it becomes a root of bitterness into our hearts; this is when we must allow the root cause of the hurt of unforgiveness to be released and forgive, so God can be forgiving to us.

This is the diagnosis to a unforgiving heart and the prognosis is to allow God's word and the Holy Spirit to correct the heart problem and release the person or persons that did the wrong, because if not it will hold us in bondage and our prayers will be hindered.

As we reflect on what a diagnosis is, we will understand how important it is to keep a forgiving heart. Let's look at the meaning of diagnosis again: it is the act or process of identifying a disease by careful investigation of symptoms, a decision reached after careful studying of facts and symptoms. In unforgiveness, we have found the fact and the symptom is a wrong suffered by an individual or individuals that is affecting how we treat them in our speech or actions. We justify holding a grudge and unforgiveness, but we don't realize it is keeping our prayers from being answered and withholding God's forgiveness to us.

The prognosis then is to forgive and let them go that our prayers can be answered and God will forgive us our trespasses.

So the meaning of prognosis is this: identifying the probable cause of a disease and how to treat the disease; the result of the treatment. The result of this treatment is to let go. Forgive so that God won't withhold any forgiveness to us and answer our prayers. We can find the answer to this in Matthew 6:9-15. It says: *After this manner pray Our Father which art in heaven hallowed be thy name, thy Kingdom come thy will be done in earth, as it is in heaven. Give us this day our daily bread, and forgive us our debts, as we forgive our debtors, and lead us not into temptation but deliver us from evil, for thine is the Kingdom and the power, and the glory forever Amen.*

The 14th and 15th verses are key. Verse 14 says: *For if you forgive men their trespasses, your heavenly Father will also forgive you.*

The 15th verse says: *But if you forgive not men their trespasses neither will your Father forgive your trespasses.*

What happens when we give our spiritual heart over to fear? Fear has torment and God hasn't given us a spirit of fear, which is just that: a spirit, and this spirit isn't of God. There is a fear of God, but it does not torment. God is love. Satan is hate, envy, strife, jealousy, malice, bitterness, unforgiving, doubt, fear and unbelief, to name a few. The devil's job is to steal, kill, and destroy.

The example of a Spiritual Fearful Heart is found below: In later pages we will give a full diagnosis and prognosis of this heart malfunction. Fear is false evidence appearing real.

This is also a diagnosis to a fearful spiritual heart and there is a prognosis to the problem. There is no fear in God. (Nehemiah 7:2) *That I gave my brother Hanani and Hannah the ruler of the palace over Jerusalem for he was a faithful man, and feared God above many.* So we are to fear God above anyone for he is our creator; there is a difference between the torment of the devil and the fear of God. In 1

John 4:18 it reads: *There is no fear in love, but perfect love cast out fear. . He that fear is not made perfect in love.*

In the same chapter verses 16 and 17: *And we have known and believe the love that God has for us. God is love, and he that dwells in love dwells in God and God in him. Herein is our love made perfect, that we may have boldness in the day of judgment, because as he is, so are we in this world Amen.*

These are just a few diagnoses and prognoses that we wanted to share to give some type of examples of how we can give a diagnosis and prognosis to our spiritual heart when there is some type of malfunctioning going on in our spiritual heart. Remembering the spiritual heart is the center focus of our spiritual makeup, because out of the abundance of our heart our mouths speak.

We must continuously be as the Lord God is asking him to create in us clean hearts and renew within us right spirits, in order to function in the upright Kingdom of God. It takes a lifetime to stay in alignment with the will of God, which is his living, breathing breath of the words that proceed from his mouth. As we come in the alignment of this living, breathing word of God, changes will take place in our hearts. There are always going to be adjustments to how we live. According to his word, this living, breathing word of God has no respect of any persons; we must be willing to come into his perfect will of his instructions and directions to live a life of pureness and holiness according to the scriptures that leads to a life of godliness in Christ Jesus the Lord, Amen.

God will cloth us with the robe of his righteousness found in Isaiah 61:10 which says: *I will greatly rejoice in the Lord, my soul shall be joyful in my God: for he hath clothed me with the garments of salvation, he hath covered me with robe of righteousness, as bridegroom decked himself with ornaments, and as a bride adorn herself with jewels.*

We must not allow the devil to condemn us. God's word will convict us and it is because of his great love for all his created beings. By doing this we can remain in the ark of safety.

Now that we have journeyed through what a diagnosis and prognosis of our spiritual hearts are and the cures of the treatments, we can discover the methods of treatment of each of these spiritual heart conditions so that healing will occur. We will discuss the methods of treating our affective spiritual heart ailments in the next chapter.

Chapter Seven

METHODS TO TREATING AN AFFECTED SPIRITUAL HEART

The Methods of Treating our Affected Spiritual Hearts

We have discovered that our spirit is the center of our lives and our spirit houses our innermost thoughts and feelings. Our spiritual heart is where all our emotions are centered such as love, hate, desire, and feelings; our soul and mind is associated with the actives of our heart. The heart is the central functioning part of our spirit man. It is out of the abundance of our hearts our mouths speak. Whatever is in our hearts the most will proceed from out of our mouths.

Since our spiritual hearts carry out our thinking process by deciding, we have been given choices by God to choose to do good or evil. God left it all up to us; we must choose who we will serve.

In order for us to discover the methods of treating any affective spiritual heart, we must find out the different types of aliments to our spiritual heart. Before we can treat our spiritual affective hearts we must diagnosis the location of the disease, and see if there is any spiritual heart murmur, spiritual heart irregularities, fearful spiritual heart, doubtful spiritual heart, spiritual heart blockage, spiritual prideful heart, unbelieving spiritual heart, spiritual uncircumcised heart, and/or spiritual heart attack. Is there any need of a spiritual heart transplant, or a spiritual heart failure? As the diagnosis is discovered, then there must be a prognosis to curing any spiritual heart problem through the name of Jesus, the word of God, and the power of the Holy Spirit, Amen.

All of the above heart problems can affect our spiritual hearts in some way in the method of treatment. We will name and diagnose each heart problem and give a spiritual prescription for the cure.

In the treatment of the methods of healing our affected spiritual hearts, we come before the Father in Jesus's name who is our Chief Physician in charge of our hearts. His assistant is the Holy Spirit, who is the intercessor, the advocate, the strengthener, the standby, the helper, the guide to rightly divide the truth in our hearts. He will search our hearts, for he is a discerner of the intents of our hearts.

We are coming before our creator in the secret place of prayer, closing out everything and focusing on what is really in our hearts and on our minds. We are asking our Father God to heal anything in our hearts that hinders us from coming before his throne boldly. The Holy Spirit will reveal these different heart problems, and in time to get our hearts in God's perfect order by aligning us with the word and the Holy Spirit.

All of these are the diagnostic tools of observation to our spiritual heart examination to the one who specializes in the impossibilities.

The type of Spiritual Heart Ailments we will deal with first is the Spiritual Heart Blockage. Spiritual heart blockage occurs when we walk in unforgiveness. This type of spiritual heart ailment will block our communication lines between the Father and his son Jesus. Unforgiveness will lead to bitterness, bitterness leads to strife, strife leads to hate, hate leads to malice, malice leads to unkindness, unkindness leads to jealousy, jealousy can lead to unbelief, unbelief can lead to fear, and fear will cause torment; all of these are attributes which is of the kingdom of darkness that comes to steal, kill, and destroy our destiny in the Kingdom of God's son Jesus who is of the Light. These are abnormal conditions of any spiritual heart that has received and accepted Jesus Christ as our savior. We must repent and let the word of God cleanse us.

The prognosis for this type of ailment is found in Ezekiel 11:19-21 which says: *And I will give one heart and I will put a new spirit within you, and I will take away the stony heart out of their flesh and give them a heart of flesh. That they may walk in my statues and keep mine ordinances and do them and they shall be mine people and I will be their God.*

Prayer: Heavenly Father, we come to you through the power of the Holy Spirit as he and the word of God examine our spiritual hearts, releasing our hearts from anything that might cause *spiritual heart blockage* such as unforgiveness, strife, bitterness, envy, jealousy, hate, malice, doubt, fear, unbelief, backbiting, or faultfinding. In the name of Jesus that can keep an open line of communication with you through the word and the power of the Holy Spirit, we release and let go of anything that would fester in our spiritual hearts in the mighty name of your son Jesus, Amen.

THE CAUSE of SPIRITUAL HEART BLOCKAGE

Spiritual Heart Blockage – What is spiritual heart blockage? Spiritual Heart blockage is caused when we hold on to envy, unforgiveness, hate, malice, strife, doubt or unbelief. It also comes from having an unclean, uncircumcised spiritual heart that refuses to change. These emotional attributes will cause the spiritual heart to be clogged up and hardened and causes rebelliousness toward the Spirit of God, refusing to hear and obey. The spiritual heart blockage can be changed if the individual will repent totally. God will change their spiritual hearts. Remember God doesn't force his will on anyone; we have to want change and turn from our wicked ways. As we turn and listen to God's word, our hearts will change, for faith comes by hearing and hearing by the word of God (Romans 10:17).

Spiritual heart blockage can also be when we don't understand how different people prosper in the world or in the body of Jesus Christ. In Psalm 37:7 it says for us to *Rest in the Lord and wait patiently for him, fret not thyself because of him who prospers in his way, because of the man who brings wicked devices to pass.* Everyone that is prosperous don't mean that the Heavenly Father has prospered them; the scripture says those who prosper in God's way means they cannot prosper by fraudulent means, underhandedness, or cheating. When God blesses his children it is through righteous means. So we must not allow anything to get in our hearts that will block our spiritual hearts from flowing in the Holy Spirit.

I thought that God had forgotten about me until I read Psalm 73:1-9 and Psalm 73: 24-28. Psalm 73:1-9 reads as thus: *Truly God is good to Israel even to such as are of a clean heart. But for me my feet were almost gone, my steps had well-nigh slipped. I was envious at the foolish, when I saw the prosperity of the wicked. For there are no bands in their death; but their strength is firm. They are not in trouble as other men, neither are they plagued like other men.*

Therefore pride compass them about as a chain, violence cover them as a garment. Their eyes stand out with fatness; they have more than heart could wish. They are corrupt, and speak wickedly concerning oppression they speak loftily. They set their mouth against the heavens and their tongues walk through the earth.

Psalm 73:24-28 reads as thus: *Thou will guide me with thy counsel and afterward receive me to glory. Who have I in heaven but thee? And there is none upon earth that I desire beside thee. My flesh and my heart fail but God is the strength of my heart, and my portion forever. For they that are far from thee shall perish; thou hast destroyed all them that go a whoring from thee. But it is good for me to draw near to God, I have put my trust in the Lord God, that I may declare all thy works. Truly am learning how to look to God and not fret because of him who prosperous in his way, my life is hide in the secret place of the most high God, and his Living word is producing his life and nature in me in this life that I can do all things through Christ Jesus who is strengthen me hallelujah Amen.*

This is the prognosis to healing spiritual heart blockage below:

It takes surrendering our spiritual hearts to the Spirit of the Most High God and his surgical tool of the word to cut out any of these negative emotions. We must allow the Holy Spirit to reveal to us how to be restored to a pure and cleansed spiritual heart. As we allow the spirit of God into our hearts, God will heal every spiritual wound so our hearts can be renewed.

Prayer: Heavenly Father we come asking you to receive our repenting heart as we recommit ourselves to the God of this great salvation to receive you in the fullness of our spirit and return to you with all our hearts washed and cleanse us from all our unrighteousness in Jesus's name, Amen.

Chapter Eight

THE CAUSES OF SPIRITUAL HEART MURMUR

Spiritual Heart Murmur

What happens in a spiritual heart that murmurs? A spiritual murmuring heart comes from negative thoughts: always complaining, grumbling, complaining about leadership: the pastors, teachers, evangelists, prophets, apostles. These people have been called for the perfecting of the ministry until we come into the unity of the faith. This is found in Ephesians Chapter 4 Verses 11-14: *And he gave some apostles, and some prophets, and some evangelists, and some pastors, and some teachers. It is for the perfecting of the saints, for the working of the ministry for the edifying of the body of Christ. Till we all come into the unity of the faith and the knowledge of the son of God unto a perfect man, unto the measure of the statue of the fullness of Christ; that we henceforth be no more children tossed to and fro and carried about with every wind of doctrine by the sleight of men and cunning craftiness whereby they lie and wait to deceive.*

God has given us pastors after his own heart found in (Jeremiah 3:15): *And I will give you pastors according to mine own heart, which will feed you knowledge and understanding.* It is not up to us to correct the leadership; God will correct them. Also found in (Jeremiah 23:1-2): *Woe be unto the pastors that destroy and scatter my sheep of my pasture. Therefore says the Lord God of Israel the pastors that feed my people, have scatter my flock and driven them away and haven't visited them, behold I will visit upon the evil of your doing said the Lord.*

This means we aren't supposed to try to correct pastors. Whatever they don't do in God's order, God called them and chose them, and he will deal with them, not us.

Jesus warned the people for murmuring in (John 6:43): *Jesus said unto them, murmur not among yourselves.* Murmuring will destroy us according to 1 Corinthians 10:10: *Neither murmur ye, as some of them murmur and were destroyed of the destroyer.* Whatever we do for the Kingdom of God should be done without murmuring and complaining; it should be done wholeheartedly, not lip service but heart service.

The prognosis of a murmuring heart is this: Don't complain, don't murmur against leadership. You'll get in trouble with God. Murmuring will destroy us. Don't murmur against yourselves; whatever our assignments from God, do it wholeheartedly. Remember, Miriam murmured and received leprosy for murmuring against Moses. Remember, keep a pure heart toward God. Always examine our hearts, think before speaking, and keep a repentant spirit. Remain prayerful and in the word of God.

Prayer: Heavenly Father, forgive us for murmuring and complaining. We ask you to help us not to be as the children of Israel going around in circles and not entering into your rest. Help us to remain steadfast in your love, your word, your knowledge, your wisdom and your understanding of who you are and what you have called us into your Kingdom to do. Help us to come up higher in your love, your peace, your joy, your goodness, your grace and your mercy. Teach us how to worship you in spirit and in truth for it is our strong weapon of warfare. When we worship you in the beauty of holiness we find the joy of the Lord is our strength in Jesus's name, Amen.

Chapter Nine

THE IRREGULARITIES OF A SPIRITUAL HEART

Spiritual Heart Irregularities

What is really meant by spiritual heart irregularities? As our natural heart experiences irregular heartbeats, we can also have spiritual irregularities in our spiritual hearts. What are these spiritual heart irregularities, how are they diagnosed, and what is the prognosis to healing?

A spiritual heart of fear brings torment and paralyzes our trust and faith in God. This Christian life is a faith walk, and faith comes by hearing the word of God. Since faith comes by hearing, then fear comes by hearing also. Since fear is a spirit and it isn't of God, it comes from the enemy of God and the enemy of our soul; this dark spirit is from the kingdom of darkness. Satan is the commander of this dark kingdom which is lord of the underworld; these fallen angels are demonic and manifestations come in various forms. They come to steal, kill, destroy, hinder, deceive, distract, plot, scheme, reap havoc, confuse, discourage, oppress and depress, cause mental torment, stress, emotional stress, and psychological torment, and also physiological problems. Fear is also an emotion. The words related to fear is to be terrified, disheartened, dismayed, tremble or dread. The familiar concept of fear will induce threatening situations such as Adam and Eve which caused them to hide from God (Genesis 3:10).

There is a fear that isn't tormenting; it is reverential to God, meaning awe, to compel, to obey, respect, to have an allegiance to God to his instructions, thus accepting his values, convictions, and behavior. God hasn't given us the torment and fear of darkness, but power, love and a sound mind, as found in 2 Timothy 1:7. God has given us weapons for warfare and in Luke 10:19 *God has given us power and authority over all the power of our enemy and nothing shall by any means hurt us; our authority and power is over serpents and scorpions and nothing shall by any means hurt us.*

We have been given the keys to the Kingdom of God that whatsoever we bind on earth or loose on earth has already been bound or loosed in heaven, according to Matthew 18:18.

God has given us the authority of his son Jesus on this earth to release heaven's atmosphere in earth's realm by speaking his creative word; this word brings the life of Jesus and heaven into the earth's atmosphere as we call those things that be not as though they are.

God's word is medicine and it will work healing inside and out of our spiritual hearts, Amen.

As I've been taught by the Holy Spirit the power of God's word, knowing that he has given me power and authority over all the power of our enemy, I am learning to stand fast in God's liberty; my prayer life has even changed. When I pray now, the scriptures just flow out of my mouth because of the learning and teachings of anointed men and women, but mostly seeking the face and purpose of God, asking, seeing and knowing, wanting more of him, and dying to myself. This is because I've learned Jesus has given me the keys to his Kingdom and power to tread on serpents and scorpions and over all of the power of the enemy, in Jesus's name, hallelujah. I have no fear of the enemy, for God's perfect love casts out the entire enemy's fear in Jesus's name.

Prayer: Heavenly Father, thank you for giving us the authority and power over all the powers of our enemy; that we can tread upon the serpents and scorpions and over all the kingdom of darkness. This spirit of fear we cast out in the name of Jesus and plead the blood of Jesus who has redeemed us by his precious blood and you have written our names down in the Lamb's book of life. You have made us free; indeed, we are no longer captive but free. We decree and declare this in the Mighty name of Jesus, the name above every name. In Jesus's name we pray that as we abide in your word and your word abides in us we know that whatsoever we ask in Jesus's name is created to bring change. There is no weapon that is formed against us that can prosper and every tongue that would rise up against us we can condemn, for this is the inheritance of the servants of God according to Isaiah54:17. In Jesus's name, Amen, so be it.

Chapter Ten

HOW TO RECOGNIZE A DOUBTFUL SPIRITUAL HEART

Spiritual doubtful Heart

What happens in a spiritual doubtful heart? When we examine a spiritual doubtful heart, it is a heart that wavers and is unstable. James 1:8 says a double-minded man is unstable in all his ways. A person with a doubtful spiritual heart wavers like the waves of the sea. Their mind is unstable. Indecision can't make up their minds; they are driven away, to and forth, wavered in their faith and trust in God's word. They are unbelieving in what God's word will do and receive no answers to their prayers. To have a doubtful heart is to be a person of two minds; it is described as one who is trusting God while trusting in something else, such as oneself or the world. We must learn to ask God in faith, believing that whatever we ask in prayer we can have by calling those things that are not as though they were in

Jesus. Someone with a doubtful spiritual heart is one who will resort to his own wisdom instead of what God provides; this is instability.

The prognosis to this type of spiritual heart is we will have to build ourselves up in the word of God through faith and belief. Having faith in God's word will move the mountain of a doubtful spiritual heart if we allow the word to purge us from this ailment.

We can learn how to call the right things of God into our lives through learning how to trust God and his word by faith. When we call on God through the power of prayer in Jesus's name it does work if we believe; we will receive by not doubting in the name of Jesus, Amen. We must allow patience to have its perfect work that we want nothing (James 1:4).

As we come to God in faith, believing that he is a rewarder to those who seek and obey him, we must diligently seek God where we might find him and he will reward our diligence. As we wait on the Lord God to heal a doubtful spiritual heart, he will strengthen and uphold us with the right hand of his righteousness (Isaiah 41:10). And in Isaiah 40:31 it says: *They that wait upon the Lord shall renew their strength, they shall mount up with wings of eagles, they shall walk and not faint.* Don't allow ourselves to get discouraged, frustrated, or unstable and not to waver in our faith. Be strong in the Lord Jesus Christ and in the power of his might, Amen.

Prayer: Heavenly Father, we come to you asking that you strengthen us from any doubt in our hearts. We don't want to be unstable and like the waves of the sea. Help us to keep our focus by continuously looking unto the hills from whence all our help comes from you, according to Psalm 121:1-3. We know you have promised to never leave or forsake us. That is what we stand on, your living word that produces your life and nature in us in this life and the ability of God is released in us now. In Jesus's name, we thank you for being our help in times of trouble and upholding us with the right hand of your righteousness in the Mighty name of Jesus, Amen.

Chapter Eleven

HOW A SPIRITUAL UNBELIEVING HEART OCCURS

A Spiritual Unbelieving Heart

What happens in a spiritual unbelieving heart? A heart that is unbelieving is lacking in faith and refuses to believe the word of God's word. In Revelation 21:8 the Apostle John wrote *the fearful and unbelieving shall have their part in the lake of fire, along with the abominable, the murderers, the whoremongers, sorcerers, and idolaters.*

This type of unbelieving heart will cause death to our soul in the lake of fire, which burns with fire and brimstones; this is the second death. I remember before getting born-again I had a vision of hell after my fourth child was born. I had an out of body experience and went to hell. This has been over forty years ago and, may I give you some information about this, I was in the church house singing in the choir but on my way to hell; you may or may not believe this, but don't take a chance. In the book of 2 Corinthians

6:14 it speaks to us to not *be unequally yoke with unbeliever, for what fellowship hath righteousness with unrighteousness? And what communion hath light with darkness?*

And in Corinthians 6:16 it says: *And what agreement hath temple of the living with idols? For you are the temple of God the living, as God hath said I dwell in them, and walk in them and I will be their God and they shall be my people.* Don't deceive yourself; God isn't marked. Whatever we sow to the flesh, we will reap the things of the flesh. The devil loves to keep us in the flesh by disobeying our heavenly Father; beware of the deceiving spirit. At one point I wasn't born-again, was fearful, and was just religious, but at 27 years old I learned that God has chosen me. Before the foundation of the world it took something drastic to turn my life around; it is described in the next paragraph.

I was sitting in the church house and singing in the choir on my way straight to hell until Jesus saved my soul. Over 40 years ago, I had an out of body experience and saw the flames of hell. It was as though I was passing through a tunnel of a roller coaster and drawing my feet back from the flames of hell. It was a dark pit, with demons everywhere. I used to not tell this experience, but I want people to know hell is real and so is heaven. Please believe this is a true experience and may you think about being true to yourselves and to our savior and Lord Jesus. To those who haven't accepted Jesus as savior, don't wait until it's too late. Please receive and accept him into your hearts. Don't go too far, stay too long, and get back and it's too late, and miss the timing of your salvation.

    I remember every detail of how I saw demons and the fire. I remember getting on my knees in hell saying, "God don't let me stay in this God forsaken place." Immediately, I awakened, crying out, "I am burning, I am burning." Don't take my experience lightly; don't be deceived or distracted by the enemy of our souls. It is past time to get our houses in God's perfect order; get ready and stay ready, when he calls you from this life or when he breaks through the sky. God has given us a freedom of choice; you must choose where you will spend eternity, no one can make that choice for you. Choose today whom you will serve. Time is winding up; think about where you want to spend eternity. In God's presence, or in damnation with the king of darkness? I made a choice to follow Jesus and I have been given a charge to keep and a God to glorify.

Prognosis to our spiritual fearful heart is to repent of fear and ask the Lord God to strengthen our heart.

Prayer: Heavenly Father, we come to you in the name of Jesus. Forgive us for any area of our hearts having in it a root of unbelief. Cleanse our spiritual hearts of any area of unbelief. We stand on Psalm 51:10, asking you Father God to create in us a clean heart and renew a right spirit within us. Have your way in our hearts as we surrender everything in this area to you. We yield to the Holy Spirit to reveal anything that's a residue that we might be purged completely. We come against the spirit of fear and unbelief in the authority of the name Jesus as we stand strong in him and in the power of his might, Amen.

Chapter Twelve

HOW SPIRITUAL HARD HEART OCCURS

Spiritual Hard Heart

What happens in a spiritual hard heart? What is the soil of your spiritual heart? It is a heart that God hasn't changed to be like his. A hard spiritual heart is a hard heart that is callous, hard to the very core of the center of our emotions. It takes a willingness to let go of all hardness which can be bitterness and unforgiveness. These are root causes of a hard spiritual heart.

A spiritual hard heart is very callous with a hard core that hasn't been broken. The ground of a spiritual hard heart must be broken up before the seed of the word of God can come in; therefore the spiritual hard heart has to be watered by the word and the Holy Spirit. What happens in a spiritual hard heart is sometimes because of how we go through trials, tests, tribulations, storms, or persecutions: this will determine the hardness of a spiritual heart. We must stay sweet and not get bitter to keep a tender spiritual heart.

We must find in the word of God a prescription of spiritual medicine that will break up and destroy the roots of bitterness and unforgiveness. There is a scripture in Mark 4:14-23; Jesus is speaking a parable saying: *The sower sows the word and these are by the wayside, where the word is sown, but when they heard Satan comes immediately and take away the word that was sown in their hearts, and these are they likewise which are sown on stony ground, who, when they have heard the word immediately receive with gladness. And have no root in themselves, and so endure but for a time and afterward, when affliction or persecution arise for the word sake immediately, they are offended. And the cares of this world and the deceitfulness of riches and the lusts of other things entering in choke the word and it became unfruitful. And these are they which are sown on good ground such as hear the word and receive it and bring forth fruit some thirty, some sixty and some a hundred.*

Everyone that is called out of the dark kingdom of Satan must fight the good fight of faith, because we have been translated into the Kingdom of God's dear son Jesus; there is a spiritual war going on now between light and darkness. We have been given a light to shine in this world against darkness; we must not hide this great light under a bushel. We must let this great light within us shine so the world will see Jesus in us; it is the candle of our soul and spirit.

Is a candle brought to be put under a bushel or under a bed? Not to be set on a candlestick? For there is nothing hid which shall not be manifested neither was anything kept secret, but that it should abroad. If any man have ears to hear let him hear. (Matthew 5:15)

Satan is our enemy. The devil is man's worst enemy; this is one enemy who wants us to believe that God doesn't love us. He is an enemy to Jesus, the church of God, and the gospel, he is tireless in his effort to uproot and sow evil anywhere he can. Satan is a murder (John8:44). He was a murderer from the beginning. These are strong words from the mouth of Jesus. The devil caused Abel to kill Cain, he also thought he had succeeded in killing our savior Jesus, but God used a secret weapon to redeem us back to himself.

God sent Jesus as a great Light into the world to bring us to the light and that we could receive this light into our hearts. When we received and accepted Jesus into our hearts, its illumination transformed us into his very image; we are now lights in the world to show others the way into the Kingdom of God through Jesus Christ our savior, Amen. This Light is a transforming light that will bring change into our lives spiritually, relationally, materially, financially, but above all eternally, by holding fast to the profession of our faith in God and his Kingdom. God's glory will be revealed in us and through us, behold our light has come and the glory of God is revealed in us around and about us. Isaiah 60:1-2. (It will be a blessing to read the entire chapter)

The prognosis to a spiritual hard heart is to hear what the Spirit of God is saying to our hearts in our spiritual ears; our spiritual ears must be open to hear the Holy Spirit. If we look at the word "heart" we can find *ear*, *hear*, and *art*. We must have a spiritual ear to hear the spirit of God speaking to our spirit man, and art is having a skill to have an ear hear what the spirit of God is saying to us in Jesus's name, Amen.

We must know our place in God's Kingdom and know the enemy of our souls and his demonic forces; we are in the mighty army of God, we must know our authority against this dark army and the power and authority that has been given us in the name of Jesus (Luke 10:19). Knowing who we are fighting is not flesh and blood but spirits of the darkness of this world and spiritual wickedness in high places. We must learn our enemies are not each other, learn the names and tactics of this dark spirit, and bind them up and render them powerless in the Mighty name of Jesus, Amen. Below we have described one of the names Satan is known as.

Satan is also known as Beelzebub – the prince of demons or prince of flies (Matthew 9:34 and Matthew 12:24). The religious leaders of Jesus's time were guilty of blasphemy against the Holy Ghost because they claimed the miracles of Jesus were actually conducted by the devil. There are many demons but only one devil, the chief leader of all the fallen angels known as demons.

The devil is known as ruler of this world (John 12:31, John 14:30, John 16:11). There are three times Jesus called the devil the ruler of this world. The devil even offered Jesus the world if he would turn stones into bread and the devil offered Jesus the kingdoms of this world. What do think the devil would offer you and me? We must be very careful and watch and pray that we be not deceived by the wicked one, in Jesus's name.

The spirit of the luminosity is the new way the devil is deceiving the church world; it means a heavenly body that gives reflection of light to a famous person, quality, condition, something luminous. This is the selling of the kingdom of the world to us; those who are lovers of themselves rather than in love with Jesus. Many are falling into this trap of building their own kingdoms and their own agendas deceiving the masses. Satan is an illuminating light that appears beautiful in appearance, bringing attention to the flesh, to self, to self-gratification; it is all about me, myself, and I. It gives no glory to our heavenly Father. This will keep us in a hardened spiritual heart. God help us to be sober minded and to wake up out of spiritual sleep.

Only through prayer, fasting and seeking God's face in truth and honesty can we break this power of darkness over our hearts and minds through the living word too. We must repent in order to be forgiven of this type of spiritual heart ailment in the mighty name of Jesus, Amen.

Stay in the word and find scripture to stand on that will identify your particular spiritual heart ailment.

The engrafted word of God encourages us. In the book of Ezekiel 36:25-26 it says, concerning a hard heart: *I will sprinkle clean water on you and you will be clean, I will cleanse you from all impurities and from idols. I will put a new heart in you, I will remove from you a heart of stone and give you a heart of flesh, and I will put my spirit in you and move you to follow my degrees and be careful to keep my laws.* We don't have to allow our hearts to be in deceitfulness of riches; the cares of the world (Luke 8:14) and the lusts of other things will choke out the word of God. We must guard our hearts; allow for good ground to be the soil of our hearts. When we open up our hearts and minds to be renewed through the word, transformation will take place in both the heart and mind.

In 1 Corinthians 10:5: Transformation starts when we learn it is not about our gifting but the presence of God and our yielding and selling out to the fullness of God. We must cast down imaginations and everything that would exalt itself against the nature of God.

We have to deny ourselves and follow after Jesus with all our hearts, minds and souls. We must trust the Lord God and not lean upon our own understanding. In Proverbs chapter 3, verses 5-6, we are told to trust in the Lord with all our heart and not to lean upon our own understanding, to acknowledge him in all our ways and he will direct our path. As I studied what condition my spiritual heart was in, this was a key scripture I used to help me to trust in the Lord and not to lean upon my own understanding, but acknowledge the Lord in all my ways that he could direct my path in the name of Jesus. These scriptures are spiritual medicines to heal any spiritual heart ailment in Jesus's name. Receive the engrafted word of God in Jesus's name, decreeing and declaring the unadulterated word of God now.

When we understand our true purpose then we will understand what transformation really is; and how gifts and callings can be without a repented spiritual heart.

We are to be transformed into the image of Jesus Christ after receiving and accepting him into our hearts. So what does the transformation involve? When we see how Jesus only came to do the will of his Father and only spoke what he heard his Father speak to him, he was obedient even until death. Jesus was tempted in all points as we are, but without any sin in his life. Our purpose is to submit to the will of God through Jesus Christ by yielding and selling out our fleshly desires to the Holy Spirit by bringing our flesh under the subjection of God through the Holy Spirit. How can we do this? It is through the transformation of our spiritual hearts. Let's look up the meaning of the word transformation according to the dictionary: the word "transformation" means to change in appearance. This happens inside first, then our outer appearance will change. It starts in the spiritual heart first and foremost. Change one form of energy into another to a higher voltage. And change in nature, especially for new use and purpose, the rearrangements of parts such as mindset and purposes.

The word of God and the Holy Spirit is the transforming substances of change, since the word of God is quick and powerful; this is the energy or voltage that empowers us for the work of God's Kingdom according to (Acts 1:8). *But you shall receive power, after the Holy Ghost is come upon you; and ye shall be witnesses unto me in Jerusalem and to all Judaea and in Samaria and unto the uttermost part of the earth.*

The amplified version of the Bible states in Hebrews 4:12 *for the word God speaks is alive and full of power (making it active, operative, energizing, and effective,) it is sharper than any two-edged sword, penetrating to the dividing line of the breath of life (soul) and the immortal spirit, and the joints and marrow (of the deepest parts of our nature) exposing, shifting, analyzing, and judging the very thoughts and purpose of the heart.*

So then this great transformation of our spiritual heart is a Supernatural process that takes place in our spirits, will rearrange how we think, speak, act and respond to this earthly life according to the image of Jesus Christ. We will learn how to live according to heaven's destiny as Kingdom Ambassadors activating the word that God speaks through our hearts, minds and mouths; this power flows from within our bellies, living water proceeding from the throne room of heaven. All of these words are the diagnosis and prognosis of a hard spiritual heart for healing.

My experiences from a spiritual hard heart to a transformed new heart came when I turned from serving Satan and the world. I had an out of body experience in 1973, in that I was in the church house, in the choir, went to Sunday School, read the Bible, but didn't know the God or Jesus of the Bible.

In 1973 after the birth of Cassandra, I was in the hospital and saw myself (spirit) coming out of my body. It looked like a dark roller coaster ride and I saw the flames of hell. I tried to pull my spirit back in my body but to no avail. I saw demons and fire, but I also saw myself on my knees in the pit of hell and when I came back into my body, I cried out, "I am burning." The people really thought I had lost my mind, but after forty-three years no one can tell me that when you die you just don't exist. Our souls will live forever in hell or in heaven; it is our choice. I made the choice. Jesus was my answer and I have never regretted it at all.

I have also had an experience since coming to Jesus Christ in 2011. I had an operation to remove gallstone. As I was getting ready to go to surgery, my daughter Ronda was in the room when the surgical technician came in to carry me down to surgery. My daughter Ronda was crying and I said, "Let's pray." I prayed that God would be with me in surgery in the name of Jesus. So the surgical technician said to my daughter, "Did you hear what your mom prayed? Her faith is in God."

Well, as the anesthesiologist put me to sleep, I saw Jesus standing in white raiment waiting to take me by the hand. We began walking around heaven; there was a high mountain with a waterfall running through it, trees, and the river of life with trees on each side. As Jesus and I stood by the river looking up at the waterfall, there was a sound of many waters coming from all of the waters of the earth. It was a voice I heard speaking to me. I understood every word spoken. The voice was coming from behind Jesus and me, giving me instructions as I had to come back to earth to fulfill my Kingdom assignment. I didn't want to come back to this earth; it was so beautiful and peaceful there. The next thing I remembered is I slowly woke up in recovery. I thought I was dreaming, speaking in my prayer language. I heard the nurse say, "Ms. Kilgore is ready to go back to her room now." I asked my daughter Ronda was I actually speaking in my prayer language? She said, "Mama you were lit up and speaking in tongues; you scared me."

There is a heaven and a hell. I have experienced them both. I don't plan on going to hell; that is for the devil and his demons and all who won't accept Jesus and the disobedient and the unbelieving. We must choose whom we will serve and where we plan to spend eternity forever; it's our choice. There is much I have enjoyed but there is a dear price to pay for living the life of Jesus Christ. Serving the Lord God is worth it all. My spiritual heart is fixed, and I'll let nothing separate me from him, nothing at all.

This is why my heart is so compassionate for living for Jesus Christ and for all to know you can recover your hearts from any spiritual heart ailments through Jesus Christ, Amen. So all we need to do is surrender to the will of God and his son Jesus which is the Living word of God. As we take up our crosses and deny ourselves and follow Jesus, if we remember Jesus was tempted as we are tempted at all points like us, but without sin. It is time to take a stand for the Kingdom of God and be wrapped up, tied up in Jesus; in other words, to be sold out for God's Kingdom. This is our ark of safety. Stay in God's presence because of what is coming on the face of this world; dark days are ahead. We need to keep our focus on the mark of the prize which is Jesus, Amen. God is our defense, our fortress, and truly God is our refuge and very present help in trouble. Believe and receive this in Jesus's name, Amen.

Prayer: Heavenly Father, it is in you we find refuge and you as our fortress to stand firmly on the word that gives life; it is the word that is alive, activates, energizes, penetrates the very core of our spiritual heart in the mighty name of Jesus. Lord we give ourselves away to you. Have your divine way as we surrender to you completely. Manifest yourself to us. We need your heartbeat, Father God, and lead us to the rock that is higher than we are. In thy dear son Jesus we decree and declare it is so in his name. Help us to count the cost for a sold-out, surrendered life to you. Please teach us how to stand in these evil days, to be steadfast, immovable, always abounding in Christ Jesus our Lord, Amen.

Read the entire 91st Psalm. It will bless your soul. This Psalm is a Psalm of protection.

Chapter Thirteen

HOW A SPIRITUAL DECEITFUL HEART HAPPENS

Spiritual Deceitful Heart

What happens in a spiritual deceitful heart? The study of a deceitful spiritual heart is to be misled by evil forces, to believe something that isn't true. It is when facts are false to delude, to trick, to beguile or to dupe another individual, an imposter, or a pretender. When our hearts are deceitful, we become a part of the master deceiver. We must get a heart examination from the great physician Jesus who specializes in the impossible.

The different types of deception that can affect our spiritual hearts are:

(1) We can deceive ourselves, which is called self-deception, self-esteem. (Psalm 36:2) *For he flatters his self in his own eyes, until his iniquity be found to be hateful, which is spiritual bondage.*

(2) Conceit (Isaiah 44:20) *He feeds on ashes a deceived heart have turned him aside, which he cannot deliver his soul nor say is there not a lie in my right hand?*

(3) Think of you only (Galatians 6:3) *For if a man think himself to be something when he is nothing he deceives himself.*

(4) Careless hearing (James 1:22) *But ye doers of the word and hearers only deceiving yourselves.*

(5) Unbridled tongues (James 1:26) *If any man among you seems to be religious and bridle not his tongue but deceive his own heart, this man's religious is vain.*

(6) Sanctimony (1 John 1:8) *If we say that we have no sin we deceive ourselves and the truth is not in us.*

(7) Spiritual poverty (Revelation 3:17) *Because thou says I am rich and increased with goods and have need of nothing and know not that thou art wretched and miserable poor and naked.*

We must prove ourselves in Jesus Christ so we don't become reprobate (Galatians 6:4). Becoming reprobate is to refuse to change in our hearts and minds; we prefer to love evil than do the will of God. Satan's rebellion was against God and iniquity was found in his heart, and when iniquity is found in our hearts because of deceitfulness, these are the things we are subject to be in bitterness: hateful, love evil rather doing God's will, full of malice, resentment, strife, witchcraft, palm reading, horoscopes reading, psychic reading, sorcery, crystal ball watchers, white magic, black magic, voodoo, worshipping of the sun, the moon and the stars, and all of which is a part of the supernatural kingdom of darkness. Don't allow your spiritual heart to be deceived by the master deceiver; stay close to the one who died for us and open up your heart totally to our redeemer Jesus. It takes being discerning, prayerful, reading up in the word, and willing to obey from our hearts, not just lip service, watching as well as praying.

We must not allow ourselves to be deceived; the craftiest of these spirits is the Spirit of Jezebel. Be very careful of this spirit. Never think you are smarter than the devil whose plots allow the Holy Spirit to lead and guide us in all the truth. Acknowledge and recognize Jesus is all powerful and all-knowing, Amen. There is a deadly spirit the kingdom of darkness uses to keep us out of alignment with the destiny of God; it is called the spirit of the Python, which comes to squeeze the very life of Jesus Christ out of us. This spirit will cut our very lifeline off if we aren't careful. It is not be taken lightly; his agenda is to get us off track doing the will of God, reminding us of past hurts and wounds, tempt us to compromise God's word, and choke the very word of God out of us. The symptoms of the python spirit are these: the attacks include wearing us out, feelings of pressure, being overwhelmed, helplessness and co-dependency. This python spirit has no respect for people; he will attack our Bible study time and our prayer life. The python spirit loves for us to gossip and complain. It is a way of distracting us from God's purpose, plan, and destiny. We must rise up in the Holy Spirit and activate our Kingdom Authority, for we have been the keys to the Kingdom of God, to bind and loose God's purpose and plan in this earth realm now. Come on, soldiers of God, take back your Kingdom Authority; we are fighting a defeated foe. Know our rightful place in the Body of Jesus Christ. It is time to take the

Kingdom back by forcing the enemy out of every area of our spiritual heart and the many members in the body of Christ, Amen.

We have to be watchful as believers because the spirit of Jezebel is very dangerous if not detected. This spirit of Jezebel enters to invade our churches by deceptive means to bring division and disunity. We must be open to the power of the Holy Spirit for a greater discernment to recognize this deceptive spirit before it tries to overtake some of the members of the body.

We must be very watchful of this spirit called Jezebel. It loves controlling people through seducing anyone in its path; from the pastor to the intercessory prayer leaders and its team members. We must beware of this takeover spirit; it tries to bring division in the church; they have a hidden agenda. There are other spirits that connect with this spirit; they are Absalom, Balaam, the spirit of Simeon, the Leviathan, wormwood, the python spirit, and the serpentine spirits. The life of the believer is to guard and keep a close watch over our spiritual hearts, resist any of these demons, and be totally committed to the Spirit of our heavenly Father.

We have been made to sit in heavenly places with Jesus Christ far above the principalities, powers, rulers of the darkness of this world, spiritual wickedness in high places, regions, and dominions of the darkness. We must be aware of false teachers and their philosophies meaning to think on their theories of men's knowledge, his own understanding of who he thinks God is, and what God is saying; this kind of wisdom is devilishly earthly, not easily treated (James 3:13-18).

It is important to know our enemy in order to examine our spiritual affected hearts so that we won't be overwhelmed by the powers of darkness. Search the scripture for spiritual medication to keep an understanding heart and keep a clearer mindset in Jesus's name, Amen. In the beginning of creation, Eve was deceived by the serpent. The serpent was more subtle than any beast of the fields that God had made.

And he said to the woman (Eve) hath God said you shall not eat of every tree of the garden? But of the fruit of the tree which is in the midst of the garden? And the woman said unto the serpent, we may eat of fruit of the trees of the garden; but of the fruit of the tree which is in the midst of the garden, God said you shall not eat or touch it lest you die. And the serpent said unto the woman you shall not surely die, for God know in the day you eat thereof then your eyes shall be opened and you shall be as gods knowing good and evil. (Genesis 3:1-5) This was one of the devil's first deceptions of the devil to humanity against God.

When God brought Eve to Adam and she disobeyed alone with her husband Adam, the devil tempted Eve and deceived her to eat the fruit of the tree of good and of knowledge. And sin entered into this world and Satan became the god of this world, but after the second Adam (Jesus being the second Adam) who took away the sins of the world, when we receive Jesus in our hearts by confession with our mouths we are no longer under the rulership of the god of this world, we are now under the systems and government of heaven. Our orders and instructions come from the Kingdom of heaven through the power of Jesus and the power of the Holy Spirit. The king of darkness is a deceiver and father of lies; it takes selling out to the spirit of God and under the microscope of the Living word that is the spirit of light that brings life and light to dead things in our lives that the devil has hindered.

In Revelation 20:10 it says: *And the devil that deceived them was cast into the lake of fire and brimstone, where the beast and the false prophet are, and shall be tormented day and night forever and ever.*

2 Timothy 3:13 reads as thus: *But evil men and seducers shall wax worse and worse deceiving and being deceived.*

It is the devil's job to deceive; the evil one will try to deceive us that we can live in sin and still go to heaven. A deceitful heart will believe a lie rather than the truth of God's word, so keep your heart under the spirit of Jesus Christ and always keep a heart to repent. The Holy Spirit who is our helper leads and guides us into all truth; this is his purpose. The Holy Spirit is our parakletos, meaning counselor, advocate and intercessor. He is our guide, the teacher of truth, and the comforter. We must trust the Holy Spirit to teach us how to rest in the knowledge of becoming all God has planned for our lives.

The first prognosis to a deceitful spiritual heart:

The Holy Spirit will uncover the plans of the deceiver and the opening up of our hearts so that we won't have a deceitful spiritual heart. The devil has many forms to try to deceive us; he is known as the accuser of the brethren, the fallen angel, our supreme enemy, and the enemy of our God too. The word Satan is a Greek word meaning false witness or malicious accuser; his wicked personality extends of evil deeds are descriptive in scripture. Example: 1 John 2:13 describes Satan as the wicked one or evil one. In 1 John 2:13, it reads as thus: *I write unto you fathers because you have known him that is from the beginning, I write unto you young men because you have overcome the wicked one.*

Satan is in opposition to everything God is and all God wants to do in our lives through us. Satan is the source of all evil and wickedness; humanity has to be delivered by the power of the name of Jesus which is the word that became flesh and dwelt among mankind. Satan can't be everywhere in all places, that is why he has fallen angels that became demons to do his bidding for souls. These demons are assigned to each person to try to keep us from coming into the Kingdom of God and entering into God's plan and purpose for our lives.

According to 2 Corinthians 4:3-4 it reads thus: *But if our gospel be hid it is hid to them that lost; in whom the god of this world hath blinded the minds of them which believe not, Lest the light of the glorious gospel of Christ, who is the image of God should shine unto them.* We have come to know there is an enemy that comes against our spiritual hearts; he works against our minds and hearts to steal, kill, and destroy.

The devil operates in the power of the air, sending havoc to hinder our walk with God.

Just as Jesus is the King of Light and his Kingdom operates in the light of the Supernatural Realm, Satan also operates out of the supernatural kingdom of darkness through doubt, fear, unbelief, deception, hindrances, strife, poverty, frustration, delusions, vain imaginations, sorcery, crystals, psychics, fortune-telling, tea leaf reading, witchcraft, and spiritualism. These describe some of the devices of our arch enemy.

Below is the prognosis:

Keep your spiritual hearts clear and alert to know the devices of the enemy; just as we know and are learning the mystery of the Kingdom of God, we must know our enemies. In 2 Chronicles 20:1-22, just a short explanation of what happened to king Jehoshaphat and the children of Judah: When their enemies came up against them and Jehoshaphat consulted with the Lord, he showed them the way their enemies were coming to attack them.

God instructed Jehoshaphat to put the worshipers before his army and they sang "bless the Lord for his mercy endures forever." It is important to know to praise the Lord God at all times, not just when trouble comes. The worship and praises will always set up defenses against our entire enemy, so keep worship and praise in your heart and mouth, in Jesus's name, Amen.

Know the devices of the enemy. These are some of the devices of our enemy:

1. Distraction - To distract us from our God-given assignments of his Kingdom business, Satan assigns

different demons to bring confusion, mental stress of all kinds to interfere and try to stop the progress of the Kingdom of God.

2. Tactics - are methods used to keep us off course of action to achieve Kingdom goals.

3. Schemes - are the secret plans, cunning plans designed to cause damage, harm, to hinder God's Kingdom plans.

4. Plots - are hostile plans to bring illegal acts or systems by strategy or strategies to succeed in a scheme.

5. Ignorance - is the biggest strategy of the kingdom of darkness's army; it is the lack of knowing the devices of Satan's dark kingdom, being unaware, inexperienced in the battle of spiritual warfare, underhanded practices of the dark kingdom's to deceive.

6. Trickery - a practice of using craftiness, underhanded tactics to deceive.

7. Deception - is the practice to mislead, misguide, act of trickery.

8. Strategies - This is a campaign against the Kingdom of God, devised plan of actions, an art of developing a warfare plan, to conduct a military attack.

We must know there are more with us than on the side of this dark kingdom, as found in 2 Chronicles 32:7-8 which says: *There are more with us than against us; with them is the army of flesh with us is God almighty.*

In Psalm 91:11 (Amplified version) God has given his angels (especial) charge over you to accompany and defend, preserve you in all your ways of obedience and service. As we continue to walk in the obedience of God's word, there will be God-given angels, who have been assigned to have especial charge over us; to accompany us wherever we are, to defend and fight for us, and preserve in all our ways of obedience and service to our God. These angels are sent to help us because we are heirs of God and joint heirs with Christ Jesus, which is found in Romans 8:17.

Prayer: Heavenly Father, please keep us from the wicked one. Do not allow us to be deceived by the treats, plots, and schemes of the wicked one, the master deceiver.

Cover us with the blood of Jesus. In the name of Jesus, we bind every wicked spirit that comes to steal, kill, and destroy in the atmospheres from the east, the west, the north, and from the south, in every region, dominion, powers of the air. In the mighty name of Jesus they are paralyzed, bound up, chained up, crushed, destroyed in the name and by the blood of Jesus, Amen.

Chapter Fourteen

WHAT OCCURS IN A SPIRITUAL DOUBTFUL HEART?

Spiritual Doubtful Heart

What happens in a spiritual doubtful heart? It is a heart of instability. The Apostle James wrote in James 1:5-8: *If any of you lack wisdom, let him ask of God, that gives to all men liberally, and unbraided not, it shall be given him; but let him ask in faith nothing wavering, for he that waver is like a wave of the sea driven by the wind, the wind and tossed, let not that man think that he shall receive anything of the Lord, a double minded man is unstable in all his ways.*

Whenever we come to God in prayer, we are to ask in faith, believing that we will receive the answers to our prayers, but a waver-minded individual has no faith to believe those things he or she asks for will come to pass, for their faith is unfruitful. We can confess the word of God all day, but we must stand in faith, believing without wavering in our faith. We have to walk by faith and not by sight.

According to the dictionary, the word waver means to move to and fro, be undecided, to hesitate, to become unsteady, and to give way.

Therefore, a doubtful spiritual heart that is waverminded is undecided, can't make up his or her mind, is hesitating in their faith, gives way to circumstances, problems, and situations, is easily shaken, moved by what is happening by their feelings and not by their faith. The word of God is that solid foundation that will not give way and is not unsteady.

The Prognosis of a spiritual doubtful heart:

A doubtful spiritual heart must learn to trust God's word by continuously hearing the word until it is established in their heart of hearts. We have given both a diagnosis and prognosis to this type of spiritual heart malfunction; now let us pray.

Prayer: Heavenly Father, we come to you to thank you for our healing and deliverance from a doubtful spiritual heart condition. Help us to see all situations, circumstances, and problems through your eyes and the power of your word in the mighty name of your son Jesus. Father God, you are truly the one who knows all the contents of our spiritual hearts. Search and know us and let no wicked way be in us. Teach us your perfect will and way in the name that is above every name. Let us keep a spiritual heart check-up daily through the leading of the Holy Spirit that searches and knows the very contents of our hearts and as we read and study your word, teach us to stand, trust, and believe that you will do exceedingly, abundantly above all we could ask or think in Jesus's mighty name, Amen.

Chapter Fifteen

THE AFFECTS OF AN UNCIRCUMCISED SPIRITUAL HEART

Spiritual Uncircumcised Heart

What happens in an uncircumcised heart? Let's find the meaning to the word uncircumcised. It means to be spiritually impure, a heathen, one who has closed their ears and heart to God, doesn't obey the voice of God or the God of all. (Acts 7:51) *Ye stiff necked and uncircumcised in heart and ears, ye do always resist the Holy Ghost as did your fathers.*

Now we shall search the meaning of circumcise: It means a surgical removal of the foreskin of the sex organ. This action served as a sign of God's covenant relationship with Abraham. And now we are in covenant with God through the blood of Jesus. Instead of the circumcision of our sex organ, God wants to circumcise our spiritual hearts.

Circumcision was the practice of the ancient world of the Jews, and the Egyptians and the Canaanites cultures. The Hebrew people performed circumcision on infants; this ritual had an important ethical meaning to them.

It is signified of people of the Jewish culture, their responsibility to serve the Holy God, who had called them in the midst of a pagan world. The first circumcision was performed by Abraham; God instructed him to circumcise every male child in his household including his servants (Genesis 17:11).

Circumcision of the Jewish male was required as a visible physical sign of the covenant between the Lord and his people. The Gentiles came to be regarded by the Jews as the uncircumcised, a term of disrespect implying that non-Jewish people were outside the circle of God's love.

The terms "circumcised" and "uncircumcised" became emotionally charged as symbols of Israel and their Gentile neighbors, that later brought discord into the fellowship of the New Testament Church.

The term "circumcision" by Moses and the Prophets was a symbol of purity of heart and readiness to hear and obey God. Through Moses, the Lord challenged the Israelites to submit to circumcision of the heart (spirit), a reference to their need to repentance, this is why we must turn to repent from an uncircumcised heart. God is calling the Body of Jesus Christ to turn from our wicked ways and pray, seeking his face and not his hand. (2 Chronicles 7:14) God's word is a surgical instrument that will cut away the foreskin of a spiritual heart to be pure. The scalpel of the word of God is as a two-edged sword that will cut away any uncleanliness from our spiritual hearts (Hebrews 4:12).

We aren't only to have circumcised spiritual hearts as a symbol of having a pure heart to serve God, but we also need to have circumcised spiritual ears to hear what the Spirit of God is saying to obey him. We must beware of what we allow in our sanctuaries; there is too much fleshly world compromising going in the house of God. The Spirit of God is being hindered as some of us are lifting up the arms of flesh more than the Spirit of Almighty God; this is idolatry.

Look at the example below as the Prophet Ezekiel speaks to the people of his day and also for us today.

In Ezekiel 44:7-9 it says: *In that you have brought into the sanctuary strangers, uncircumcised in heart and uncircumcised in flesh, to be in my sanctuary, to pollute it, even in my house, when you have offered bread, the fat and the blood and they have broken covenant because of all your abominations; and ye haven't kept the charge of mine Holy things, but ye have set some keepers of my charge in my sanctuary for yourselves. Thus said the Lord God, no stranger, uncircumcised in heart is among the children of Israel.*

We have polluted the house of God with our own agendas and entertainment and not worshipping the Lord in spirit and in truth. We have brought into our sanctuary people who have not received the Lord God into their hearts, musicians and even praise song leaders contaminating and polluting God's sanctuaries.

God's presence can't come in as he desires to, because we are calling the pulpit a stage and performing instead of having the fear of God and reverence in his holy temple. The anointing can't come because of our disunity and not being on one accord quenching the Spirit of God. We think we are on a program to entertain the people to focus on the arms of flesh as we put our own agendas in place; calling it God is just a trick of the devil, rocking God's people to sleep through man's philosophies and rituals. The anointing isn't there, so how can people be delivered and made free?

God desires to deliver his people and really set and make them free, but because of some quick meals of some type of sermon we've made up, because we haven't studied the word nor spent time in the presence of God to hear from heaven to feed God's sheep. We neither have repented, nor consecrated ourselves for the service of the Lord; and there is no anointing to destroyed yokes. God wants the refreshing wind of the Holy Spirit to purge all this worldly junk out of his way. The body of Jesus is in need of a spiritual heart overhaul. To cleanse our uncircumcised heart from the ways of the world we need to turn from these wicked ways and repent; let God purify our hearts again.

In Isaiah 43:18-19 it reads: *Remember ye not the former things, neither consider the things of old. Behold, I do a new thing, now shall it spring forth, shall ye not know it? I will even make a way in the wilderness, and rivers in the desert.*

God has sent Jesus so that we can dwell in the fullness of his Spirit through the reconciliation of his blood on the cross. We were sometimes alienated by wicked works, *yet now hath he reconciled; in his body of his flesh to present you holy and unblameable and unreproveable in his sight* (Colossians 1:21-22). We have to be aware *lest any man spoil you through philosophy and vain deceit after the tradition of men, after the rudiments of the world, and not after Christ.*

(Colossians 2:9-14) *For in him dwell all the fullness of the Godhead bodily. And ye are complete in him which is the head of all principality and power. In which also ye are circumcised with the circumcision made without hands, in putting off the body of sins of the flesh by the circumcision of Christ. Buried with him in baptism, wherein also you raised with him through the faith of the operation of God, who hath raised him from the dead. And you being dead in your sins and the uncircumcision of your flesh, hath he quickened together with him having forgiven you all your trespasses. Blotting out the handwriting of ordinances that was against us, which was contrary to us, and took it out of the way, nailing it to his cross.*

God is doing a new thing; if we would ask him for a modern day upper room experience where miracles, signs, and wonders can take place without anyone laying hands on us, there are intercessors and watchman on the wall crying out for a latter day move of God to breathe on the people of God; who want to see a latter rain fall into the Body of Jesus by repenting and turning from all our wicked ways. There is such a hunger for souls, and purified hearts, a commitment to service, God in spirit and in truth. The only way this can happen is to get this uncircumcised heart ready by the cutting away of the foreskin of the sins of compromise and complacency, men's philosophies, the rudiments of the world, men's own agendas and building of their own kingdom of the world.

We are still talking about the uncircumcised spiritual heart; these are the things God dealt with me about my spiritual heart. This word is not just for the members of the Body of Jesus Christ, this word was given to me first. It is a message and word that I had to be the first partaker of. I am so passionate about my spiritual heart as well, for other brothers and sisters in Christ Jesus, please don't take these words lightly; it is a message straight from the throne room of God. As we seek the face of God waiting in his presence to hear from heaven, be still and learn the direct voice of our savior. Listen as he speaks to your spirit, and then obey; you will be a changed person. We all need to grow more in the grace and knowledge of God. None of us have arrived; it is more to come from being in God's presence. Wait on the Lord God in prayer. The winds of change are really blowing. Get ready, get ready, we haven't seen nothing yet.

This is the first prognosis to an uncircumcised heart:

We need to wait in the presence of God; in prayer, seek his face and his Kingdom, asking for a revival of our hearts. We must be prepared for the new wind and the greater awakening in the spirit. This requires us to surrender our spiritual heart to the potter and allowing him to have his way in the spirit realm, through fasting and prayer; don't forget the studying of his word.

God wants to circumcise our spiritual hearts according to Psalm 51:10. To create a clean heart and right spirit, this requires this surgical scalpel of the word to cut away the foreskin of sin from our uncircumcised heart.

God is calling us up into a higher place in him in the spirit realm to be in total alignment with the Supernatural light of his Holy Spirit to see by 20/20 supernatural eyesight and to have fresh anointed ears to hear what the spirit of God is saying to his body of believers in this final hour. We must position ourselves according to his plan and purpose for his Kingdom work. A fresh new wine of the Holy Spirit is needed to be more empowered because of shifting and binding the powers of darkness, yet if we are too low in the sprit realm the demons will take advantage of weak believers. We must be strong in the Lord Jesus and the power of his might.

We must drink of the refreshing wine in the spirit and this new wine is giving us the Supernatural Power to do the greater works Jesus spoke of in the book of John. In our final examination of the uncircumcised spiritual heart, let's look at how the Prophet Jeremiah gives warning to the people in his day; it also applies to us in the twenty first century. (Jeremiah 6:10) *To who shall I speak, and give warning, that their heart may hear? Behold, their ear is uncircumcised, and they cannot hearken, the word of the Lord is unto them a reproach, they have no delight in it.* God is speaking through these pages of this book. Give your ears and heart to his warning, that we may hear what the Spirit of the Lord is saying to his churches, surrendering our whole spiritual heart to the Father.

God is speaking to all dominations; he is a God of no respect of color, nationality, origin, or different nations, but a God of all creatures of the earth, mankind in general. We need circumcised ears to hear in the spirit realm. The word of God says he that have an ear hear what the Spirit is saying to the church. When we look at the word's heart we can see, hear, and art. The spiritual heart has an ear to hear what the

Spirit of God is saying and it takes an art or skill to hear God speaking; this means our ears must be sensitive to hear the voice of God and his sheep know his voice and strange voices they will not follow. Amen.

We must not be dull of hearing what God is speaking to his Church and to the assemblies of churches; to have uncircumcised ears is to be insensitive to the voice of God. To have circumcised spiritual ears is to hear and obey the voice of God. We must know who is worshipping. Jesus spoke to the woman at the well and said these words: you don't know who you worship. Read it for yourself in John 4:22: *Ye worship ye know not what, we know what we worship, for salvation is of the Jews.*

Now that we are believers in Jesus Christ, we too know who we worship. Ask the Holy Spirit to give you the Revelation of this passage and he will. God is calling us to a more intense prayer life and dwelling in the secret place of the most high God; come up in the spirit realm. Just as the Spirit of God invited John on the island of Patmos to come in the spirit realm, he saw and heard mysteries. We can too; just listen to what the Spirit of God is saying, Amen.

Final prognosis to an uncircumcised spiritual heart is to be circumcised inwardly that an external sign can shine the light of God to those still in darkness to bring them into the Kingdom of God. God wants to circumcise our spiritual heart according to Deuteronomy 10:16: *Circumcise therefore the foreskin of your heart and be no more stiff-necked.*

We get in and stay in the presence of God, purified by the blood of Jesus in our hearts that the work of God can be manifested, and we can truly give God all the glory due his name. Our devotion is to him and circumcision is essential to our Christian faith and fellowship with God and one another as we build the Kingdom of God and our Christ.

This is the way I have been able to keep my spiritual heart circumcised by the Holy Spirit. To do spiritual surgery on my heart continuously with the scalpel of the word of God, it is what we call purging our spiritual heart, another way of cleansing the spiritual heart. The word purge means to make clean from impurity in the figurative sense of cleaning from evil; purity or purification is a state of being or process of becoming free of inferior elements or ritual uncleanness. To be ritually pure means to be free of some flaw or uncleanness, which would bar us from a Holy God. We must have a purified spiritual heart to come before a Holy God.

Purity relates to cleanness of heart, mind and soul; it is a person who is in the right relationship with God. To live a life of purity, the blood of Jesus has cleansed us from all our sins. To have a circumcised heart is to have a continuous cleansing of the spiritual foreskin of our hearts from sin by repenting and releasing anything in our hearts not like Jesus Christ.

Prayer: Heavenly Father, we ask you to cut away the foreskin of our uncircumcised heart that have anything that isn't like you, that our hearts may be purified from any sins of commission or omission. In the name of Jesus, wash us thoroughly with the living word of God that we may use to bring glory to your mighty name. Pour forth your love in our hearts and keep our hearts and minds in the mighty name of Jesus, Amen.

Chapter Sixteen

HOW A SPIRITUAL HEART ATTACK HAPPENS

Spiritual Heart Attack

The causes that leads to spiritual heart attacks:

This chapter is basically about how a spiritual heart attack occurs in the life of a believer. It involves all of these irregularities of the spiritual heart, which are spiritual heart murmur, spiritual doubtful heart, spiritual uncircumcised heart, spiritual unbelieving heart, and spiritual heart blockage, to name a few.

If these spiritual heart conditions aren't dealt with, it can lead to a spiritual heart attack. The spiritual heart is very delicate, because out of the abundance of our heart (spirit) our mouth speaks. The heart must be guarded with all diligence, for out of our hearts flows the issues of life (Proverbs 4:23). We have found that each of the spiritual heart ailments have issues. For example, the uncircumcised spiritual heart has impurities; where the foreskin of the spiritual heart has to be cleansed by the surgical scalpel of the word of God, the word of God is sharper than any two-edged sword, energizing and penetrating the very soul to the dividing line of the deepest parts of our breath of life and the immortal spirit.

Since we act and think from our hearts, and our spiritual heart is the center of the functioning of our spirit man, we must watch the words we speak; it will create an atmosphere of positive or negative plans for our lives. Remember life and death is in the power of our tongues (Proverbs 18:21). When we don't keep a guard over our spiritual hearts, the issues in our lives sometimes get uncontrollable if not dealt with immediately by the word.

Spiritual heart attack stems from not exercising our spiritual heart muscles and our authority as believers, which is meditating on the word, studying to show ourselves approved by God, workmen not being ashamed, rightly dividing the word of truth, not being a hearer of the word, not allowing the word to penetrate our spirit to the engrafted word of God for purification of our spiritual heart, not allowing the word of God to be a strong two-edged sword in our mouths, not using the keys of the Kingdom of God and our power and authority in the name of Jesus, allowing the cares of this world and the deceitfulness of riches and the lusts of other things to enter in and choke the word and it becomes unfruitful (Mark 4: 19).

When we allow the cares of this world and the deceitfulness of riches to choke the word of God out of our hearts, we are inviting a spiritual heart attack in our lives; it will take us into spiritual heart failure if we don't humble ourselves through fasting and seeking God's face for real and stop playing the demonic game of the devil's deceitfulness, for God knows our hearts.

Spiritual heart attack can also be caused by staying in unforgiveness, having your heart hardened through rebellion, doubt and fear of man. Spiritual heart attack certainly occurs when the love of God has seeped out of our hearts; this is when we allow our spiritual hearts to wax cold; we won't repent, forgive our brothers and sisters, and hold grudges. The love of God in our spiritual heart is the center valve to pump through our hearts the love of God and all we do for the Kingdom of God.

Without God's love, we are sounding brass and tingling cymbals; we are just noise makers (1 Corinthians 13: 1-13). *Though I speak with the tongues of men and of angels, and have not charity (love), I am become as sounding brass, or a tinkling cymbal. And though I have the gift of prophecy and understand all mysteries, and all knowledge: and though I have all faith, so that I could remove mountains, and have not charity, I am nothing. And though I bestow all my goods to feed the poor, and though I give my body to be burned, and have not charity, it profit me nothing. Charity suffers long, and is kind, charity is envy not, charity vaunted not itself, isn't puffed up, don't behave itself unseemly, seek not her own, isn't easily provoked, think no evil, rejoice not in iniquity, but rejoice in the truth, bear all things, believes all things, hope in all things, endures all things, charity never fails, but whether there be prophecies, they fail cease, whether there be tongues they shall cease, whether there be knowledge, it shall vanish away. We know in part, and we prophesy in part. But when that which is perfect is come, then that which is in part shall be done away. When I was a child, I spoke as a child, I understood as a child, I thought as a child, but when I became a man, I put away childish things. For now see through a glass, darkly, but then face to face, now I know in part, but then shall I know even as also I am known, and now abides faith, hope, charity, these three, but the greatest is charity.*

This is why the spiritual heart without God's love will not profit us anything. Love is the key which holds us together with the Father, for God is love. His love never fails. Without God's love spiritual heart attack is inevitable.

This is one of the prognoses for healing the spiritual heart of a spiritual heart attack:

In 1 John 4:7-19 it says: *Beloved let us love one another for love is of God; and every one that loves is born of God and know God. He that loves not, know not God for God is love. In this was manifested the love of God toward us, because that God sent his only begotten son into the world, that we might live through him. Herein is love, not that we love God, but that he loved us, and sent his son to be the propitiation for our sins. Beloved, if God so loved us, we ought also to love one another. No man hath seen God at any time, if we love one another, God dwells in us, and his love is perfected in us. Hereby know we that we dwell in him, and he in us, because he has given us his Spirit. And we have seen and do testify that the Father sent the son to be the Savior of the world. Whosoever shall confess that Jesus is the son of God, God dwells in him, and he in God.*

And we have known and believe the love that God hath for us, God is love: and he that dwells in love dwells in God and God in him. Herein is our love made perfect, that we may have boldness in the day of judgement: because as he is, so are we in this world. There is no fear in love, but perfect love cast out fear, because fear has torment, he that fear is not made perfect in love. We love him because he first loved us. Amen.

HOW A NATURAL HEART ATTACK OCCURS VS SPIRITUAL HEART ATTACK

In comparing the natural heart attack to a spiritual heart attack, let's see how a natural heart attack can occur: In the natural heart, heart attack occurs when the blood flow is cut off, forming a clot within the coronary artery to a section of the natural heart.

In a spiritual heart attack, when the love of God becomes clogged up by bitterness, unforgiveness, doubt , fear, or unbelief, we become spiritually dead; we cut off the Spirit of God's life which is his love, we become backslidden in our minds and then in our hearts. It will take deliverance from this type of heart condition and much prayer and fasting.

When a spiritual heart attack occurs, we will need some spiritual resuscitation; this means our spiritual hearts need to be revived.

What do we mean by the word resuscitation? According to the dictionary, to resuscitate is when a person is unconscious, not able to think or feel, not aware of their surroundings, the part of the mind not directly or fully aware of thoughts, feelings, or ideas. When we lose the love of God, our desires change from loving God to the things that pleases our flesh. We no longer desire to pray, read about

God, praise and worship God; our minds become bogged down with worries, anxieties, stress, and financial problems, and the cares of the world. We need to be brought back to the life of Jesus and the cross. Some of us have lost our consciousness of thinking with the mind of Christ Jesus, have lost our feelings of compassion for the lost and destitute, not being aware of the spiritual warfare and the spiritual surroundings, allowing human nature to take place over the spirit man, and our thoughts and desire for the King and his Kingdom no longer interest us in pleasing our heavenly Father.

We need the breath of God and his son Jesus to do mouth to mouth spiritual resuscitation. We are unconscious of our feelings of caring and loving one another; we have lost our zeal for Jesus Christ; some of us, not all of us. In the medical field to resuscitate is called CPR, which stands for cardiopulmonary resuscitation, or the kiss of life, or mouth to mouth resuscitation. We all need some spiritual resuscitation to bring us back to the divine purpose and life of Jesus Christ. Some of us have lost our focus and purpose for lifting up the name of Jesus and need to stop and think; it is not about us being famous or talking about our ministries, our people, when we are God's people and his sheep. We need to allow Jesus to give us some cardio-spiritual resuscitation, the kiss of the Holy Spirit, breathing the reviving life support of Jesus in our spiritual lungs to bring us back to the fullness of God and his work in us. The Kingdom of God is all about King Jesus and the work of the Father God breathing his breath into our spirits once again to ignite us with the Mighty Power of the Holy Spirit; working the work of him who says *go I send thee to compel the lost to come in the ark of safety.* We need to talk about the Father and his son Jesus by lifting up the word of God that doesn't change; obeying the Father from our hearts and not just lip service, speaking only as the Holy Spirit gives us the words to speak as Jesus did; he spoke only what he heard the Father speak.

Jesus came neither talking about himself, but about his Father and his Father's Kingdom. Jesus spoke only what he heard the Father saying and obeyed.

We need to recognize all these things that we named that have caused so many spiritual heart attacks in the Body of Jesus Christ and there is need of some strong resuscitation in our spiritual lives. Since the love of God seeps out, it is because our spiritual heart arteries have been clogged up and waxed cold. These are things that happen when God's love waxes cold in a spiritual heart; we get void of the thirst and hunger for God and his word, lose our intimate fellowship with God and other believers, backslide in our hearts and minds, void of witnessing the gospel to the lost, become stubborn and rebellious, prideful, hateful, unforgiving, self-deceptive, believe a lie rather than truth, gossip, backbite, controlling in situations, self-righteous, holier than thou, and manipulative. All of these things will lead to a spiritual heart attack, blocking the flow of God's spirit in us, and will stop up our worship and praise to God.

We have to go into prayer, visiting with the resuscitator of our abundant life support, Jesus. When Elisha did the first resuscitation on the boy in 2 Kings 4:32-35 he went into the house, and behold the child was dead, and he put his mouth upon his mouth and his eyes on the child's eyes, his hands upon the child's hands, then he stretched himself upon the child, and the flesh of the child waxed warm, the child sneezed seven times and he opened his eyes.

Jesus wants us to keep our hands in his hand, wants us to drink into the spirit, breathe into our nostrils of the breath of fresh, resuscitating life, to revive us, restore us, set us on fire with the Holy Spirit, bring us out of our unconscious state of mind, be focused on what is going on in the realms of the spirit, get our charge to keep back, and glorying the God of our charge to fulfill our callings, serving Lord God in spirit and in truth. The breath of God is that same breath that breathes life into Adam and Adam became a living soul. God gave us the second Adam, Jesus, to bring us back in fellowship with the Father, that we can complete our mission of bringing others into his Kingdom, that they may experience this life-giving breath of God's creative power to bring change into the earth's atmosphere.

God is listening for each of our heartbeats to get in rhythm with his heartbeat. God wants to release unlimited love, peace, joy, mercy, grace, compassion, goodness, relationships, and finances, putting us back in total spiritual heart health as we become willing and obedient (Isaiah 1:19). This is the prognosis to a spiritual heart attack.

Prayer: Father God, we come asking you to restore and revive our spiritual heart from a spiritual heart attack through resuscitating us back to the life of your son Jesus Christ, that we may be renewed back to our first love through communion and fellowship as you and your son come to make your abode with us. As we seek you and your Kingdom and all your righteousness, we surrender every part of our spiritual heart to you in Jesus's name, Amen.

We all go through a time of a spiritual heart attack, when our spiritual heart almost fainted in a trial, test or persecution. My spiritual heart became faint when my three children each passed at different times. I am not saying I understood what was going on, but in each journey God kept me. When I went through each situation my spiritual heart almost fainted, until it was almost over, then I realized God had strengthened me in ways I couldn't see until it was all over.

Now I realize it was to strengthen my faith and to be a testimony to others who may go through the same situations or similar circumstances or problems. It has been through these circumstances I now know it was to learn how to have compassion for others and to show the love of God as he has given us a loving and understanding heart of his wisdom and strength. There is nothing too hard for God and there is nothing impossible with God and us as we believe. I am still learning from the word of God how to turn everything over to him and to stand on the rock who is Jesus, and he is the rock that won't give way to tests, trials, persecution, or storms. Jesus is the foundation to our faith as we build our hope on nothing less than Jesus Christ and his righteousness. Amen.

Chapter Seventeen

HOW TO RECEIVE A SPIRITUAL HEART TRANSPLANT

Spiritual Heart Transplant

What happens in a spiritual heart transplant? A spiritual heart transplant starts with repenting and confession to Jesus Christ with our mouths and believing in our hearts (Romans 10: 9-10). *That if thou shalt confess with thy mouth the Lord Jesus and shall believe in thine heart that God hath raised him from the dead, thou shall be saved. For with the heart man believe unto righteousness and with the mouth confession is made unto salvation.*

It takes confessing to Jesus Christ with our mouths and believing in our hearts to have a spiritual heart transplant; when the heart is transplanted, we receive a new way of living.

In the beginning, God created man in his image and likeness, he breathed the breath of life into his nostrils and man became a living soul. In (Genesis 1:26-27) *And God said let us make man in our image, after our likeness and let them have dominion over the fish of the sea and over the fowl of the air and over cattle, over all the earth, and over every creeping thing that creep upon the earth. So, God created man in his own image, in the image of God created he him, male and female created he them.*

As we read the 27th verse of Genesis, God created male and female. Have you ever noticed this? God spoke the word *let us make man in our own image and likeness*. When God named Adam, his name means humanity or mankind, so when Adam sinned, humanity sinned. This is why all of us without Christ Jesus have sinned and fallen short of the glory of God. The first Adam, representing all creatures after his kind to cause a sinful nature to enter into the earth realm; Adam had the first spiritual heart attack.

Therefore the blood of goat, turtledove, and other animals was used as a sacrifice for sin. When the second Adam, Jesus, came to redeem us back to God by the shedding of his blood, this was for the remission of our sins. Jesus is the lamb that took away the sins of the entire world and all who would accept him into their hearts would become new creatures. God had already devised a plan to redeem humanity from the treason of the evil plan of the devil. The blood sacrifice of Jesus was the holy purifying, sanctifying, cleansing, washing away the sins of humanity, and all who would accept God's only begotten son as Savior and Lord over their lives. There is nothing that can cleanse us from sin but the blood of Jesus.

This is the first and only way to receive a spiritual heart transplant; it was in the plan of God to restore mankind back to full fellowship with him. Jeremiah 29: 11 says: *I know the thoughts that I think toward you, says the Lord thoughts of peace, and not of evil, to give you an expected end.* The expected end is to receive salvation through Jesus Christ to be one with the Father and his son, to have fellowship and communion, and be one with our brothers and sisters in Christ Jesus.

God sent his only begotten son Jesus to reunite us back to fellowship and communion with the Father through the shedding of his son's blood. When Jesus died and was resurrected from the dead, all mankind has a right to eternal life through the death of the cross. Now because of Jesus we are made the righteousness of God by the blood of Jesus, our hearts are transplanted through our belief, confession, and trust in who Jesus is, and we become as he is righteous, so are we made righteous.

God desired that our hearts be transplanted through this scripture; Jeremiah 31:33 reads as thus: *but this shall be the covenant that I will make with the house of Israel, after those days said the Lord; I will put my law in their inward parts and write them in their hearts and will be their God, and they shall be my people.* We have been given a new covenant by the blood of Jesus; we are blood-washed, blood-redeemed, blood-cleansed, and have a blood covenant with the Father because of the blood of Jesus.

When our hearts are transplanted, God gives us a new heart (Ezekiel 11:19): *I will give them one heart (a new heart) and I will put a new heart within them, and I will take away the stony heart (hardened heart) out of their flesh, and I will give them a heart of flesh (meaning a changed, sensitive, responsive heart) the touch of their God.* To have a transplanted heart is to change by having God's heartbeat for intimacy, fellowship, praise, thanksgiving and worship with the lover of our souls. Without the love of God there will be no sensitivity to his heartbeat, and our spiritual heart will have an abnormal rhythm for the heartbeat for God and his people. When our hearts are transplanted, we become new in our hearts and minds; true change takes place when we begin to worship in spirit and truth, giving our whole heart in an intimate fellowship with the lover of our souls.

PRESCRIPTIONS FOR SPIRITUAL HEART TRANSPLANT

This is the Prognosis for spiritual Heart transplant:

Psalm 51:2 *Wash me thoroughly from my iniquity, cleanse me from my sin.* Psalm 62:5 *My soul wait thou only upon God, for my expectation is from him.*

Psalm 61:4 *I will abide in thy tabernacle forever, I will trust in the covert of thy wings.*

Psalm 63:4 *Thus will I bless thee while I live; I will lift up my hands in thy name.*

Psalm 27:1 *The Lord is my light and my salvation of whom shall I fear, the Lord is the strength of my life of whom shall I be afraid.*

Psalm 57:7 *My heart is fixed, O God, my heart is fixed, and I will sing and give praise.*

I remember the transformation of my spiritual heart transplant over 40 years ago. I am amazed at how God continues to grow me in his grace and knowledge of who he is through the Revelation of his word. As I remember the words of Kenneth Hagan and his radio program saying, "never become unteachable," what I've learned is no matter how long you have had a transforming experience to this salvation, there is always something new to learn and experience. In this journey you never can think you know it all or have arrived in Christianity.

Always keep a hunger for God and his word, remain humble, steadfast and unmovable, always abounding in the word and work of the Kingdom of God. Stay in the love of

God, growing in the grace and knowledge of Jesus Christ; be strong in the Lord Jesus and in the power of his might. Through the years I've come to know each growth in the Lord Jesus is an increase in our trust and faith. Loving to dwell in the secret place of the most high God is where I love to be, because no foe of ours and Lord God can stand before him or us. Standing on the foundational rock of salvation, no storm can withstand as we trust the Lord with all our hearts and not lean upon our own understanding (Proverbs 3:5-6).

It is important to read and really study the word of God and allow it to get in your heart (spirit) and minds. I love to hear the word speaking back to my spirit confirming what God has said to me in my intimate time of prayer, praise, and worship.

In Deuteronomy 30:14-16 *But the word is very nigh unto thee, in thy mouth and in thy heart, that thou my do it. See I have set before thee this day life and good and death and evil. In that I command thee this day to love the Lord thy God to walk in his ways and to keep his commandments and his statues and his judgements, that thou may live and multiply and the Lord thy God shall bless thee in the land wither thou go to possess it.*

As we allow the word of God to penetrate our spiritual heart it transforms us into the image of Jesus daily to be like him; we enter into the promises of God by believing every verse and line of the life-giving, activating word that gives us abundant life to live according to God's perfect will.

We have many precious promises from God; every verse and line of his word is instructions to a promise if we stand on it. There is a word for every situation we go through; there is an answer. When we put the word in our spiritual hearts and in our mouths, we can get good results by remaining in his word, it will not return to him void (Isaiah 55: 11). Each scripture given can be a blessing to you spiritually and you can use them for your own personal Bible study or meditation for prayer and worship. This is my very passion, the love of God and his word, and his people to see them grow in spirit and faith.

Prayer: Heavenly Father, we come thanking you, for whoever reads this portion of this book may receive a spiritual heart transplant by receiving and accepting Jesus into their hearts; let the entrance into your word to bring light into their very souls, to enlighten their eyes and mind of understanding in the mighty name of Jesus, Amen.

Chapter Eighteen

WHAT HAPPENS WHEN SPIRITUAL HEART FAILURE OCCURS

Spiritual Heart Failure VS Natural Heart Failure

Heart failure in the natural heart is developed after other conditions have damaged or weakened the heart. It can also occur if the heart becomes stiff. In heart failure, the main pumping chambers of the heart (ventricles) may become stiff and not fill properly between beats; your heart muscle may become damaged and weak. Over time the heart can no longer keep up with the normal demands placed on it to pump blood to the rest of the body.

What happens to a spiritual heart in heart failure? In spiritual heart failure, the love of God is blocked out. It gets hardened and causes the love of God to dry up, causing the spiritual heart to get bitter, mean and cold hearted. The heartbeat of God stops flowing with the love of God and the love the believer once knew becomes cold, angry, and bitter with God and others, turning back to the things of the world, slowly, until they become backslidden in heart and mind. A spiritual heart that experiences the loss of God's love becomes stubborn, prideful, self-righteous, self-deceptive, self-gratifying, a liar, void of the hunger and thirst for God, controlling and manipulating.

This is when Satan brings seven other demons back in and the state of the person is worse than before salvation. As they continue to turn away from God and his love, Satan will gain access to our spiritual heart and mind; we will open the door for the kingdom of darkness and other spirits to enter in our spirit man. Matthew 12:43-45 says: *When the unclean spirit is gone out of a man, he walks through dry places, seeking rest and finds none. Then he says, I will return into my house from whence I came out; and when he is come, he finds it empty, swept, and garnished. Then goes and takes with him seven other spirits more wick than him, and they enter in and dwell there: and the last state of that man is worse than the first. Even so shall it be also unto the wicked generation.*

It is the job of our enemy of our souls to cause us to give up on God and our salvation. We must remember to keep our mind in captivity with the mind of Jesus Christ. If not, the devil is looking for some way to enter back into our spiritual hearts. The devil knows how to battle us in our minds because the mind is the battlefield. If we open our minds to the thoughts of the devil, he will bring and keep bringing entertaining thoughts; we cast them down and out every vain imagination in the name of Jesus. We must learn how to fight those evil thoughts through the word of God. 2 Corinthians 10:4-5 says: *For the weapons of our warfare aren't carnal but mighty through God to the pulling down of strongholds. Casting down imaginations, and every high thing that exalted itself against the knowledge of God and bringing into captivity every thought to the obedience of Christ.*

As believers, we must cast out of our minds any thoughts that are not like Jesus; we have to allow this mind that is in Christ Jesus to be in us according to Philippians 2:5. And each day *be renewed in the spirit of our minds* according to Ephesians 4:23. This takes a constant reminder of studying the word of God daily to keep our minds renewed.

These scriptures are a part of our prognosis to spiritual heart failure. As we position ourselves to recover our spiritual hearts from a spiritual heart condition there must be some instructions to follow by our Great Physician Jesus. It is this: Colossians 3:2-16

Verse 2: Set your affection on things above, not on things on the earth

Verse 3: for you are dead, and your life is hid with Christ in God.

Verse 4: when Christ, who is our life shall appear, and then shall you also appear with him in glory.

Verse 5: mortify, therefore your members which are upon the earth, fornication, uncleanliness, inordinate affection, evil concupiscence, and covetousness which is idolatry.

Verse 6: for which things sake the wrath of God comes on the children of disobedience.

Verse 7: in which you also walked some time, when you lived in them.

Verse 8: but now you also put off all these: anger, wrath, malice, blasphemy, filthy communication out of your mouth.

Verse 9: lie not one to another, seeing that you have put off the old man with his deeds.

Verse 10: and have put on the new man, which is renewed in knowledge after the image of him that created him.

Verse 11: where there is neither Greek nor Jew, circumcision nor uncircumcision. Barbarian, Scythian, bond nor free but Christ is all and in all.

Verse 12: put on therefore as the elect of God, holy and beloved bowels of mercies, kindness, humbleness of mind, meekness, longsuffering.

Verse 13: forbearing one another and forgiving one another, if any man Has a quarrel against any: even as Christ forgave you, so also do you.

Verse 14: and above all these things put on charity, which is the bond of perfectness.

Verse 15: and let the peace of God rule in your hearts, to which also you are called in one body and be you, thankful.

Verse 16: let the word of Christ dwell in you richly in all wisdom: teaching and admonishing one another in psalms and hymns and spiritual songs, singing with grace in your hearts to the Lord.

Prayer: Heavenly Father, we thank you for showing us how to recover from spiritual heart failure by allowing you to resuscitate and massage our spiritual heart muscle and by breathing a fresh word into our spirit. As you teach us through the power of the Holy Spirit to submit to you with all our hearts and to draw closer to you by having an intimate love affair with the love of our souls, we give you glory, honor and praise in Jesus's name, Amen.

Chapter Nineteen

RESUSCITATION OF A SPIRITUAL HEART

What occurs when a spiritual heart is resuscitated?

In our journeying through the different parts of our spiritual heart, we must get in the realm of the Spirit of God, allowing the Holy Spirit through prayer to help us accept the diagnosis of our spiritual hearts and receive a prognosis for the cure. As Jesus and the Holy Spirit is allowed to examine our spiritual hearts to see what has affected any area of these spiritual heart conditions: spiritual heart blockage, spiritual heart murmur, spiritual hard heart, spiritual uncircumcised heart, spiritual heart failure, spiritual heart attack, spiritual heart transplant, and how a spiritual heart can be recovered from any these spiritual heart diseases and some of the spiritual heart irregularities in a spiritual heart, that is out of the love of God to name a few. As we seek God for spiritual heart resuscitation, we must come into intense intercessory prayer seeking God's face and all his righteousness. God wants to breathe on us by the blowing winds of the breath of life to revive and resuscitate us to the powerful life of Christ Jesus the Lord, Amen.

When our spiritual heart is in need of some spiritual resuscitation, it is because the fire and anointing has burned out. The fire of God needs to be rekindled. In order to rekindle the Holy Spirit's fire, we must be ignited through prayer, praise, the word of God, and worship. When our minds are in need of resuscitation, we are bogged down with worry, frustration, sometimes doubt, fear and mistrusting God, we need to get back in faith and confidence, and we need to repent.

We have become unable to have compassion for the word and for sinners; our thinking is off; we become passive in our feeling for others; the cares of the world have overtaken the ways of the Kingdom of God; and we come down from the wall of intercession of praying for our nations and standing in the gap for others. We need the resurrected power of Jesus Christ to fill us with the wind of the breath of life; this is our resuscitation back to living the life of Jesus, and will restore us back to his resurrected power to bring glory to God.

The Holy Spirit is the power that will release the unlimited Supernatural power of heaven that we might do the work that has been assigned for us to do on planet earth. In the book of Genesis 1:26: *and God said let us make man in our own image, after our likeness and let them have dominion over the fish of the sea and over the fowl of the air and over the cattle and over all the earth and over every creeping thing that creep upon the earth.* Genesis 2: 7: *and the Lord God formed man out of the dust of the ground. And breathed into his nostrils the breath of life, and man became a living soul.*

God created male and female; he created Adam in his likeness and image and breathed his breath into the man's (Adam's) nostrils, and he became a living soul; but when Adam and Eve sinned, they brought sickness, disease and death into the earth's realm for all humanity. Adam experienced the first spiritual attack that resulted in spiritual heart failure.

When Jesus, who was the second Adam representing all humanity, Jesus's life represented spiritual heart resuscitation, uniting us back to the life of God through the shedding of the blood of Jesus. It is because God the Father sent his only begotten son Jesus into the world because he so loves us. God so loves the creatures he created in his likeness and image, he sent Jesus to give us life more abundantly and the Holy Spirit to quicken our spirits by empowering us for service.

All of us at one point need some type of resuscitating, when we sin and fall short of the plan and assignment of God. When we except Jesus into our hearts he comes in to revive our spiritual hearts back to spiritual health. Jesus is our life supporter that gives us spiritual life to live a holy and acceptable life in the sight of God in this life on earth.

In Psalm 57:7 it says: *my heart is fixed, O God, my heart is fixed: I will sing and give praise*. This is the procedure that will help lead us to help resuscitate our spiritual hearts. God has breathed in our spirits through the fresh wind of the Holy Spirit; we can change our atmospheres by bringing the heavenly realm of heaven to the earth. When we call on the name of the Lord Jesus in spirit and in truth, we can call those things that be not as though they were. Romans 4:17 says: *As it is written, I have made thee the father of many nations before him whom he believed even God quicken the dead and call those things which be not as though they were.*

Since Abraham is our spiritual father and we have been engrafted with the Jews by Jesus renting the veil of the temple from top to bottom, the two have become one, Jew and Gentile. We have been made the righteousness of God through Jesus Christ; we have been given power to call those things that are not as though they were. For example, if you are sick and diseased, (Psalm 103:1-5) we can *bless the Lord O our souls and all that is within us; who heals all our diseases and forgives all our iniquities, Who satisfies our mouths with good things and renews our youth lie the eagles.*

We can call our healing into our bodies and call our finances healed by paying tithes and offerings, giving to the poor and needy in the name of Jesus. All of this is a part of being resuscitated spirit, soul, mind, body, relational, and financial; it is what the Bible calls being in health even as our souls prosper: (3 John 1:2) *Beloved I wish above all things that thou may prosper and be in health, even as thou soul prospers.*

God wants us to prosper and be in health as our souls prosper, and we must surrender our whole hearts to God. We must give ourselves away completely, sell out to his Holy Spirit, and not allow idolatry to take the place of the Living God in our hearts. We must have a total heart transformation by allowing the fullness of the image of Jesus to transform us into his very likeness. We must not be bound by the spirit of the pharaoh and the spirit of Egypt. We all go through the wilderness experiences, but in the desert there is a well of living water flowing out of our bellies to empower us to go through in Jesus's name, hallelujah, Amen.

We must not allow the old things of the past to keep us bound by a slave mindset of bondage; we must keep our mind and heart free of old mindsets in order to move out with the heartbeat of God. We have been made to sit in heavenly places with Christ Jesus far above principalities, powers, might and dominion and every name that is named. (Ephesians 1: 19-21, Ephesians 2: 6)

Ephesians 1:19-21 reads as follows: *and what is the exceeding greatness of his power to us-ward who believe, according to the working of his mighty power, which he wrought in Christ, when he raised him from the dead and set him his own right hand in heavenly places. God set Jesus far above all principality, and power and might, and dominion and every name that is named, not only in this world, but also in that which is to come.*

In Ephesians 2:6 *God has raised us up together in heavenly places in Jesus Christ.* We must know how to take and use our authority and allow the Spirit of God to lead and guide our footsteps in Jesus's name, Amen.

This is the prognosis for a resuscitated spiritual heart:

As God continues to refresh our spiritual hearts by breathing in us and on us, we have the Holy Spirit to keep us empowered even in the wilderness and desert places in our lives. Our wilderness is our place of preparation, to get all the impurities out of our spiritual hearts and minds. The wilderness and desert places are places of revival, restoration, a place of renewal of our spiritual hearts to develop pure love for God and his people. The wilderness and desert is a lonely place, a place to get our focus back on our first love. We need to get back our desires to please the one who called us out of the kingdom of darkness into the Kingdom of the Light of Jesus, back to prayer and fasting; something will only be delivered out of our lives through fasting and prayer. God wants us to get reacquainted with him through repenting, retraining us in spiritual warfare, redeveloping us from spiritual breakthroughs, and repositioning us in his place of Authority and Power of the Holy Spirit to work Supernatural miracles, signs, and wonders.

God has given us keys and power through the endowment of the Holy Spirit; according to Acts 1:8 we have received power after we are filled with the Holy Spirit to do the work of the Kingdom.

In the wilderness we receive how to activate our Kingdom authority, and as we thirst and hunger from the very presence of God in a Supernatural acceleration to stand in the liberty of Jesus Christ. In the wilderness we learn the very heartbeat of God and we learn to stand on all his promises that are in him, Amen. As we relate to Jesus's wilderness experience, this experience happened after Jesus was baptized and the Holy Spirit drove Jesus into the wilderness to be tempted by the devil.

In Matthew 4:1-11 Jesus was led up by the Spirit into the wilderness for forty days and nights and Jesus was hungry. The devil tempted Jesus by asking him to turn stones to bread, but Jesus answered the devil by saying *man doesn't live by bread alone but by every word that proceed out of the mouth of God*. Jesus always gave to the devil what is written in the word of God. When we are in our wilderness experiences, we must also give our enemies, the devil and his demons, the written word of God. As we remember there is so much power in the word of God and the name of Jesus, the name that is above every name, Amen.

There is a song that says every beat of my heart is for you. God's heart beats for the fellowship and love of his children who have come into his son Jesus's Kingdom and those we will usher into the Kingdom as a harvest of souls. We are no longer in bondage to Egypt and the pharaoh; we have freedom through the blood of Jesus, and we are free indeed. We all will go through a wilderness or desert experience which is a dry place to prepare us to be strong in the Lord Jesus.

I remember my wilderness experiences and how I had a vision of being in the wilderness, but there was a giant spring of water coming out of the sand and the Holy Spirit spoke these words to me: "The water is me, the Lord God, in the midst of this vast, dry desert of a wilderness. You will never be without my presence in the midst of a dry place, for I the Lord God has promised never to leave you nor forsake you. That is my promise to you. I AM with you wherever you go; you aren't alone. Press into my presence for I Am your refuge and fortress, your God, your heavenly Father. Trust me."

It is easy to have a joyful heart when everything is going well, but what do we do when these things occur: Our money is funny, the well is dry, the bank account is in overdraft, the light bill is due, and the pantry is almost empty? It is then we must still praise and trust God for everything we have need of. Remember, God is in the midst of our greatest and deepest wilderness experience; we have to still be able to trust him. In my wilderness experience I had to still lean totally on trusting God for my deliverance, standing still to see his salvation. My thirst for God was still in my wilderness dry desert place; my thirst for God was even greater.

Therefore it is still a daily journey with me to lean, to rely, and depend on Abba Father who sees and knows all things, especially my spiritual heart, and to let go and allow God to have total control of every thought and beat of my heart in Jesus's name, Amen. In my journeys on this Christian walk, I often wondered why I knew different things before they would happen. Even as a child I had dreams, saw different things; for a long time I wouldn't tell them. When I was about eleven years old I had a dream; at the time I didn't know it to be a vision. In this dream I was now an adult and some of my neighbors and classmates were out partying and drinking; we had an accident and hit a telephone pole. We all died. There was no funeral, but we all ended up in the cemetery. There was the devil and every time he would raise his hand, one of my neighbors would go down in the ground.

As I am writing this, God is giving me the revelation of what it meant. I heard the Holy Spirit saying they were lost and the devil had them. I don't know how I knew this was the devil, all I know is he was black as anything I ever saw. His teeth were so white and he looked at me and said, "I am going to get you." I said, "No you will not." I don't know why I was the only one with a lavender robe on. When the devil said "I am going to get you," I looked up in the sky and this was the very first time I remembered seeing Jesus, and when I looked up I began to rise up to meet him in the air. His nailed, scarred hands and feet, I saw, and his white raiment with a red shawl around his chest. I am almost sixty-seven years old and that has been fifty-six years ago; it was really amazing now that I think of it. God had this all planned before I was conceived; it was in his divine plan of God, Amen.

This has been my resuscitating, refreshing spiritual journey as the Lord God breathes the fresh wind of his Spirit in my spiritual lungs and breathes in my spiritual nostrils new discernment to be skillful and fruitful for the up building of his Kingdom in Jesus's name, hallelujah.

As I continue this journey, I am reminded of the strength test I took while in college; it was called the Clifton Strength Finder Quest. It amazed me to find that my strengths are strategic ones. The professor had us write what our strengths were. Below is what I wrote for the paper.

I often wondered why there were times where I perceived something happening without giving thought. It was just discernment; guiding my inner feelings was the still, small voice of God the Father; guided by the path he was leading me to go. I needed to learn not to lean on my own understanding but to acknowledge God in all my ways so he could direct my paths.

I remember when I got born-again, seeing a vision of me walking a narrow walkway with lights on each side; it reminds me that the word of God is a lamp unto my feet and a light unto my pathway.

As I learn my strengths are a part of the plan of God before the foundation of the world, the first strength is restorative and has caused me a lot of dismay until I discovered it has given me confidence in whose I am and who I've been chosen to be and to do for God's Kingdom. Jesus's resuscitating life support is keeping me balanced and teaching others as I learn to be disciplined. My other strength is empathy; I have always suffered because of God's compassion in me for helping in the medical field, the mentally challenged, and physically challenged. This emotion has surrounded me most of my life. I am learning everything is not as serious as I have made them, and I am learning to evaluate the situations and circumstances, leading of the Holy Spirit with godly solutions through the word of God.

The developer strength causes me to see the potential in others to view no individual by my own opinion. I wondered why different people have been drawn to me discussing their personal problems; it is because the Lord has drawn unsaved people to hear the message of salvation and my testimonies.

The connected strength has allowed me to understand the reason things happen. It is because of my purpose God has for my life. The assignment that God has given me to complete before he calls me home or Jesus comes back, whichever comes first. It is God given talents that were born in me and are being developed in order to finish the course of life. God has given me and others a free- will; that doesn't mean we do things that isn't lined up with his will, which is his word.

We are all going to be stretched to grow in God's grace and the knowledge of Jesus Christ. We must have clear vision to see in the spirit realm, Amen.

I am learning how to communicate to others, being sensitive to their needs, and having the compassion of the Lord Jesus, being sensitive to their feelings too. We have to stand on the word of God no matter who likes it or not. You may have to stand alone sometimes when we speak the word of God in love and in truth. Integrity will carry us a long way. All through life's journey, hold on to God and let him hold you in the palm of his hand. Everyone won't drink the same type of tea you drink; it depends on how thirsty we are for righteousness of the Spirit of God like you. Some people are sent in our lives by the devil; we must discern who comes from our enemy of our souls, to distract, to hinder our walk with the Lord, or to sabotage our steadfastness in the word, faith, praise, worship and prayer.

This is why my strength of adaptability - not to look back at my hurts and pains, but to overcome them through faith in God, moving forward on this journey, as Phyllis learns to adapt to different circumstances, planning to succeed in asking God to help me to stand in the evil day. To be strong in the Lord Jesus Christ and in the power of his might, stay in the love of God, be still and know he is God, to stay in the washing of the word and under the blood of Jesus, using the name Jesus which is a name above every name in heaven, in earth, and beneath the earth. Keep a heart full of the love of God to love the unlovable and the downtrodden. Keep breathing the resuscitating Spirit of Life in me daily in the name of Jesus.

Prayer: Heavenly Father, we come to you asking that you refresh our spiritual heart by restoring us back to the life that you gave us when we received Jesus as our savior. We want him not only to be our Savior but Lord over our lives. Let the refreshing winds of the Holy Spirit blow and fill us to overflowing, to empower us to work the work of your Kingdom, in the mighty name of your son Jesus, Amen.

Chapter Twenty

RECOVERING FROM A SPIRITUAL HEART ATTACK

How to recover from a spiritual heart attack

As we have journeyed to our appointment with the Great Physician Jesus and his assistant the Holy Spirit, by allowing him to examine our spiritual heart, learning about the irregularities and aliments of our spiritual heart, we have found a spiritual heart can go into spiritual heart murmur, spiritual doubtful heart, spiritual heart failure, spiritual uncircumcised heart, spiritual heart transplant and how we can recover a spiritual heart from a spiritual heart attack. There are many diagnoses and prognoses for curing all of these different hearts conditions and recover from a spiritual heart to a healthy spiritual heart.

There are spiritual medications found in the word of God for healing any of these ailments to our spiritual hearts. God's love will heal any wounds or pains that occur in our spiritual hearts and spiritual heart issues. We must remember there is nothing too hard for God, and to those of us who will stand believing his word, nothing will be impossible for us.

Jesus came to resuscitate us back to the life God gave to us in the beginning; now we have been restored back to a more abundant life through the shedding of his blood and the new covenant with the Father through the son, Amen. When we repent and accept the new birth, Jesus changed our entire life step by step, second by second, minute by minute, and hour by hour, then we are given one day at a time. We will never accelerate overnight in the kingdom of light; we grow in grace and in the knowledge of Jesus daily as we spend quiet meditation, prayer, and the living word of God. We must never come before God without thanksgiving, praise and worship; this brings the presence of God in our atmosphere to have an intimate fellowship and communion with the Father, the son, and the Holy spirit. This is a love session of intimacy with our Father God. Through praise and worship we give ourselves to God as living sacrifices. This is the season of restoration and a great awakening to the Spirit of Jesus Christ and our God; we must be yielded vessels for the glory of God the Father. We must surrender our hearts totally to him and let him have control in Jesus's name, Amen.

We are being prepared to meet the King of kings and Lord of lords. It is past time to get our houses in God's order and sell out completely; this means to recover our hearts from any spiritual heart conditions that might be affecting our obedience to the word of God and Jesus Christ. We need to be living sanctuaries, holy and acceptable unto God. There is a song that says *Lord prepare me to be a living sanctuary pure and holy, tried and true to be a sanctuary Lord for you.* God is calling us to get our hearts in tune with his heartbeat, following the leading of the Holy Spirit, to do the assignments and plan of the Kingdom as ambassadors of his Kingdom, representing our King Jesus. The secret place of the Most High God should be our dwelling place, seeking his face and his Kingdom and all his righteousness. The inner sanctuary of our spiritual hearts is where the very core of our spiritual life begins, where only God resides in the holy of holies, a place of fulfillment in him, and the intimacy of a love affair with our God.

Come go with me into the secret place of the Almighty God and feel the refreshing wind of the Holy Spirit to revive, to resuscitate, and to restore our spiritual heart by recovering our hearts to a healthy spiritual heart condition to the work of the Kingdom.

Some of us need a spiritual heart transplant; we have allowed the enemy to rock us to sleep, our hearts have become hardened, some of us have become lovers of ourselves more than lovers of God. God is calling us back to holiness, sanctification, prayer, laying aside all of the weights that are easily besetting us; our mindset needs to be changed, we have wrong motives, wrong attitudes, mean, bitter, and some of us are just plain nasty. We need a heart transplant very badly. The people of the world can't tell the difference between the saved and unsaved.

God has to change our spiritual hearts to make a difference in the world but not of this world; we are to be a part of HIS HEAVENLY KINGDOM.

God wants all our hearts and he desires praise, thanksgiving and worship; when we do these things it will change the atmospheres, and miracles, signs, and wonders will take place; but we must be ready and stay ready, by having the preparation of our hearts. (Proverbs 16: 1-3) *The preparation of the heart in man, and the answer of the tongue, is from the Lord. All the ways of a man are clean in his own eyes: but the Lord weights the spirits. Commit thy works unto the Lord, and thy thoughts shall be established.* When we commit our thoughts to God it will be established and so shall our ways. As Proverbs 3: 5-6 says: *trust in the Lord with all thy heart and lean not upon your own understanding in all your ways acknowledge him and he will direct your path.*

These are the spiritual medication prescriptions to recover from any form of heart conditions if used correctly. When we acknowledge God in all our ways, he will release unlimited blessings, health, wealth, prosperity, love, joy, peace, goodness, mercy, compassion, unlimited provisions, and revelation, knowledge, and truth. This is why it is so important to grow up spiritually first. As 3 John 1:2 says: *beloved I wish above all things that thou may prosper and be in health even as your soul prosper Amen.*

We must wake up and be sober in these days that are evil; it is not the time to have spiritual heart failure, or a spiritual heart attack, but if you do there are always answers from the word of God and the Holy Spirit, help to cure those ailments.

We have to wake up from drunkenness of the cares of the world, manipulations, controlling spirits, mind blinding spirits, mind bogging spirits, the python, the serpentine spirits that are the cobra, rattlesnake spirit, the spirit of ignorance of the devices of the devil, distraction, deception, condoning sin, self-gratification, self-centeredness, greed, lusts of the flesh, respect of persons, cliques, slothfulness, idol worship, the lifting up of the flesh more than God the Father, palm readers, spirit of divination, psychics and the like. The serpentine spirits are the cobra which sows discord; it poisons relationships and spreads lies. The rattlesnake is a gossiper and busybody. We must beware of all serpentine spirits.

We need to clean up and stop playing with our salvation, get our hearts right with God, for he knows our hearts. There is no secret God doesn't know; stop fooling ourselves. We may ask ourselves what these things have to do with recovering from a spiritual heart attack; it is imperative to know what has caused the spiritual heart attack in the first place and any of these spiritual heart conditions.

All of these things must be cut out through the cutting off of the foreskin of our spiritual heart that is sinful to the nature of God. As we continue to press into the presence of God, the Holy Spirit will reveal anything that is in our spiritual heart that is out of alignment with the word of God. He will cleanse and purify the areas that needs to be washed by the Living word that sifts, analyzes, penetrates, energizes, and exposes the very deepest part of our spiritual hearts (Hebrews 4:12).

God refreshes our thoughts through the mind of Jesus Christ, because the things of the world vie for our attention to keep us off focus of the things of the Spirit of God. We must have a stable relationship with the Father, the son Jesus, and the Holy Spirit to be one with the three, which is the whole trinity of the God head. As we stand still and see the salvation of the Lord we must allow God to be our refuge and help.

Psalm 46: 1-11 says: *God is our Refuge and Strength (mighty and impenetrable to temptation). God is a very present and well-proved help in trouble.*

Verse 2: Therefore we will not fear, though the earth should change and though the mountains are shaken into the mist of the sea.

Verse 3: Though its waters roar and foam, though the mountains tremble at its swelling and tumult, Selah (pause and calmly think of that)

Verse 4: There is a river whose streams shall make glad the city of God, the holy place of the tabernacles of the Most High.

Verse 5: God is in the mist of her, she shall not be moved: God will help her right early (at the dawn of the morning).

Verse 6: The nations raged the kingdoms tottered and were moved: He uttered His voice, the earth melted.

Verse 7: The Lord of hosts is with us; the God of Jacob is our Refuge (our Fortress and High Tower) Selah (pause and calmly think of that)

Verse 8: Come; behold the works of the Lord, who has wrought desolations and wonders in the earth.

Verse 9: He makes wars to cease to the end of the earth: He breaks the bow into pieces and snaps the spear in two; He turns the chariots in the fire.

Verse 10: Let be still and know recognize and understand that I Am God. I will be exalted in the earth,

Verse 11: The Lord of hosts is with us; the God of Jacob is our Refuge (our High Tower and Stronghold). Selah (pause and calmly think of that) What a Mighty God we serve; when we think of that calmly how God so love us so that he wants to keep our spiritual hearts recovered from any of these spiritual heart conditions and especially a spiritual heart attack. (Amplified Version)

As we learn God is our help, because of him we can have refuge, our only fortress and high tower, our very help in trouble. We must remember in this world we will have trouble; we must be of good cheer because Jesus has overcome the world that we can be more than overcomers. (John 16:33) We serve the God of Abraham, our spiritual father; his sons Isaac and Jacob are his descendants and so are we. Abraham is our father of faith and as he believed God and was his friend; as we learn to trust God and his word we become his friends also.

We can behold the works of our God in every circumstance, situation, heartache, troubling agent, all that we encounter on life's journey, with faith in the Lord Jesus. Remembering God is our strong tower and we can pull down every stronghold because God is our Strong Tower and very help in trouble, Amen.

As we can all relate to God's Spirit, and we are regenerated into the image of his son Jesus. No man can see God and live, but we must learn His Spirit. How do we get to know God's Spirit? We get to know God's Spirit through communion, having an intimate fellowship through prayer, and the word of God. When we come into the presence of God with thanksgiving, praise and worship, we enter into his gates with Thanksgiving and into his courts with praise we are thankful unto Him and bless his name (Psalm 100: 1-5).

When we enter into the presence of God expecting to receive all that we need to live a godly life in this present-day world; through being strengthened in our hearts and minds in the word and prayer, leaning on our solid foundation Jesus the Christ, Amen.

We as God's people must seek his face and not his hand. 2 Chronicles 7:14 asks us to turn from our wicked ways, to pray, and we will hear from heaven and God will heal the land.

This is how we can receive resuscitation and revival to our spiritual hearts, which needs to be brought back to the fullness of abundant living for Jesus Christ; by allowing Jesus into our spiritual tabernacles to restore our spiritual hearts and recover the JBPORRR (which stands for Jesus Christ Power of Resurrection, Restoration and Revival to the God head.

None of us can come to the Father but through Jesus Christ and there is no other way whereby we can enter into his Kingdom. It took the Resurrected power of God for Jesus to get up out of the grave and all power was given him in heaven, on earth, and beneath the earth, and he has given us this same resurrected power according to Luke 10:19. We have power and authority in the name that is above every name. Jesus is the name above every name and everything is subject to his name. We have everything we need through the name and blood of Jesus. In Luke 10:18-19 it says: *and He said to them, I saw Satan falling like lighting (flash) from heaven. Behold I have given you authority and power to trample upon serpents and scorpions, and (physical and mental strength and ability) over all the power that the enemy (possesses): and nothing shall in any way harm you. (Amplified Version)*

The power we have been given is our authority to the Kingdom of heaven and our God. We have been given the keys to God's Kingdom and whatsoever we bind on earth or loose on earth is already bound or loosed in heaven (Matthew 16:19). You see, it is imperative what we speak comes out of our heart through our mouths. Matthew 15:18 says *but whatever comes out of the mouth comes from our hearts, and this is what makes man unclean and defiles him (amplified version).* So if we are speaking the word of God as given, we are made clean. In the King James Bible Matthew 10:19 says: *Behold I give you power to tread on serpents and scorpions and over all the power of the enemy and nothing shall by any means hurt you.*

See how powerful the word of God is? When we put it in our hearts and in our mouths and believe what it says, things will happen in the atmospheres and in the realm of the spirit. This is how we keep a recovered heart by staying connected to the word of God, believing and holding fast to what we read as the Holy Spirit teaches us to live according to these powerful words.

Jesus promised the disciples of old he would send a comforter who would be an advocate, a strengthener, an intercessor, a standby, a helper, and he would bring things to our remembrance; this is the refreshing wind that is blowing to empower us for greater works for the King and his Kingdom in Jesus's mighty name, Amen.

In order to keep and recover our spiritual heart, we need to be sober in mind and thoughts; we must know the source of our enemy by being watchful (1 Peter 5:8). It is a principal for our instruction for spiritual training by casting all our cares, worries, all our anxieties, all our concerns once and for all on the Lord Jesus, Amen.

We are in a spiritual battle with Satan's kingdom of darkness against the Kingdom of God and his son Jesus's Kingdom of light, so he is after our heart (spirit) and we must guard our hearts diligently for all our issues proceed from the heart to our mouths; therefore we must guard our hearts. We must yield our hearts, souls, mind, and bodies to the Spirit of the Living God; it is the only way to bring our bodies, souls, minds and spirits under the subjection of the Holy Spirit and obedience to God.

As we commit to the will of God and focus on our authority and use the word as a key to being more than conquerors through Jesus Christ, then we can be watchful of the enemy of our souls by standing our ground against his onsets. We must be vigilant and cautious at all times, knowing that the devil roams around like a roaring lion, seeking whom he might devour, but we have to resist him and give him no place. The word of God lets us know to commit to God; resist the devil and he will flee, so we must learn to stay in tune and committed to the one who has called us out of the devil's kingdom into this marvelous light of the Kingdom of God's son Jesus.

Our minds must be sober and we must stay alert, aware of the spiritual realms of darkness and of the spiritual realm of light of God's Kingdom. Our focus is on the authority of the word of God and the power that is in Jesus; remembering that greater is Jesus Christ within us than the (devil) that is in the world.

When we stay in the presence of God by acknowledging he is the true source of our lives; sitting in his presence by being still to hear his instructions for each day he gives us to complete our daily assignments for the King and his Kingdom. As we commune in prayer and the word of God will carry us through each second, each minute, each hour and we will have completed the entire 24 hours of one day.

We must take one day at a time. God is in control of our lives if we allow him to be the source of all we have need of; when we allow him to walk in the garden of our hearts it becomes a sweet fellowship of intimacy. God has given us a garment of righteousness; we are made in the righteousness of God through Jesus Christ our Lord by his shed blood. We have the confidence of knowing we are in the acceptable year of the Lord and he has granted us consolation and joy to those who mourn in Zion to give us an ornament (a garland or diadem) of beauty instead of ashes, the oil of joy instead of mourning, the garment (expressive) of praise instead of heavy, burdened, and failing spirit that they may be called oak of righteousness (lofty, strong, and magnificent, distinguished for rightness, justice and right standing with God. (Amplified Version) This is the garment of praise that the Joy of God gives us our strength, it empowers our spirits to lift our voices so the spirit of mourning can be broken and destroyed as we stand in righteousness, justice and right standing with our God; knowing no weapon formed against us is able to prosper and every tongue that would rise up against us, we can condemn in Jesus's name, Amen.

We must remember the word of God is a working medicine; God has given his word, a name that is above every name which is Jesus. This is how powerful his name is. Since the word of God is a healing medicine it can bring health to all our spiritual heart ailments and its conditions. The King James version of the Bible speaks in Proverbs 17:22 concerning our heart like this: *A merry heart does good like a medicine: but a broken spirit dry the bones.* Nehemiah 8:10 says: *then he said unto them go your way, eat the fat and drink the sweet and send portions unto them for who nothing is prepared: for this day is holy unto our Lord: neither be you sorry, for the joy of the Lord is your strength.*

We find that because God's joy strengthens us, it works healing to our spirit man and God wants our entire being to be healthy according to 3 John 1:2 *Beloved I wish above all things that you may prosper and be in health even as your soul prospers.* Jesus is the healer of every part of our being. He paid the price that we might live this life in abundance; the more we eat and digest the word of God, the more our hearts are filled with Jesus and God's glory, Amen. As we stay in God's presence, his love, joy, and peace overflows our spirits and it works healing in every part of our lives. These are spiritual medications found in the word of God for healing and making our spiritual hearts to be cheerful and bringing the joy of the Lord to strengthen every area of our lives in Jesus's name, hallelujah.

As we surrender to the Spirit of God, he will recover all our spiritual heart ailments and the issues of the root causing our heart conditions. The Holy Spirit will bring an igniting fire to our hearts by the indwelling power of the Holy Spirit. The Seed of the word of God has been implanted in our spiritual hearts to make us fruitful and to multiply a harvest of souls for the Kingdom of God. We are pregnant with Jesus and he is being formed through the word that is in our hearts; it is when we become full of Jesus through prayer along with the seed of the word, we will produce a great harvest of souls because we present Jesus and his Kingdom and not ourselves. It is all about Kingdom building for our Lord God and King Jesus; as Jesus spoke of the Father and said what the Father spoke to him, we are to be one with Jesus and the Father, that we speak only what the Holy Spirit is speaking to us as we continue to change into Jesus's image, Amen.

As we surrender to the Lord Jesus and remain in the secret place of the Most High God, whose power no foe can withstand, we will be inaccessible in the secret place and see the reward of the wicked (the kingdom of darkness) and those who have made the devil their god. Remember we found that Jesus is resuscitator to us, to bring us back to his life and mindset; he is breathing a refreshing flow of his Spirit, massaging our spiritual heart muscles, bringing us to consciousness of his Kingdom of light, making us conscious of the Supernatural Realm of his Kingdom of Light and the power he has given us to stand strong in him and the power of his might.

God is breathing into our spiritual nostrils, which is spiritual discernment, sharpening our discernment to recognize the powers of darkness more clearly. We must be ready to take by force what the enemy has taken from the Kingdom of God. Rise up, people of God. Take your ordained places in the Kingdom of God's son Jesus, Amen. Allow the Spirit of all creation to recover our spiritual hearts from a spiritual heart attack through the Living word and prayer.

Chapter Twenty-One

THE KEYS TO RECOVERING AND KEEPING A SPIRITUAL HEART

In recovering our spiritual hearts we must keep a heart of repentance; we can easily sin in words, thoughts, actions, in spirit, and in our deeds of the flesh. We must not be of the systems of the world or allow our fleshly carnal nature to dictate to our spirits. We must stay in the love of God, deny ourselves, take up our crosses, and follow Jesus all the way to glory. We must meditate in the word day and night to have the success plan of God and not lean on our own understanding, but acknowledge God in all our ways. (Proverbs 3:5-6)

Joshua 1:6-8 says for us to *be strong and of a good courage, for unto this people shall thou divide for an inheritance the land, which I swear unto their fathers to give them. Only be thou strong and very courageous, that thou may observe to do according to all the law, which Moses my servant commanded thee: turn not from it to the right or to the left, that thou may prosper withers ever thou go. This book of the law shall not depart out of thy mouth, but thou shall meditate therein day and night, that thou may observe to do according to all that is written therein, for then thou shall make thy way prosperous and then thou shall have good success.*

We must stand for righteousness, not to compromise the word. God has given us everything that pertains to living a godly life in Christ Jesus the Lord. As we live according to the prescriptions of the word of God, it becomes healing medicine for our hearts, souls, minds, and bodies. It will keep us with some healthy spiritual hearts of recovery. The word of God will balance our lives to his righteousness and our purpose of his Kingdom. God will teach us through the Holy Spirit to walk according to his plan. Jeremiah 29:11 says, according to the Amplified version: *For I know the thoughts and plans that I have for you, says the Lord, thoughts and plans for welfare and peace and not for evil, to give you hope in your final outcome.* God knows our lives from beginning to end; we must stand complete in Jesus and God's plan of salvation. It works.

God always watches over his word and performs it. It will never return to him empty according to Isaiah 55:11 which says: *So shall My word be that goes out My mouth: it shall not return to Me void (without producing any effect, useless) but it shall accomplish that which I please and purpose and it shall prosper in the thing for which I sent it.(Amplified version)*

When we remind God of his word, he will perform it as we speak it back to him; this is why it is so important to see where we have allowed any of these spiritual heart conditions to cause us to go into spiritual heart attack or spiritual heart failure. Spiritual heart attack and spiritual heart failure are very important parts of our spiritual hearts; they both can be recovered.

In spiritual heart failure, it takes repenting and forgiving. In spiritual heart attack, it takes allowing the word of God to give us a spiritual heart massage and Jesus resuscitating us by blowing his life back into our spiritual lungs. This is recovering our hearts from the attack.

God is waiting for those of us who have experienced a spiritual heart attack to recover, to be restored back to the life of his son Jesus Christ. Come back, backslidden sons and daughters, to the lover of your souls. God has need of you. God is married to the backsliders and there is nothing we can do that is so bad that God won't forgive us; this is why he sent Jesus, because he so loves the world and the creatures he made in his image and likeness, he doesn't want anyone to perish. Our hearts have been recovered from sin's grip through the shedding of the blood of Jesus, and the confession of our faith and believing in our hearts. We have the authority to stand and to do all to stand in the liberty of Christ Jesus our Lord and King.

We must remember no weapon formed against us will prosper and every tongue that would rise up against us, we can condemn in the name of Jesus (Isaiah 54:17). The word of God is near us in our hearts and in our mouths; we have to speak it forth and believe it. Deuteronomy 30:14: *But the word is very nigh unto thee in thy mouth, and in thy heart that thou may do it.* This same word is found in Romans 10:8: *But what saith it? The word is nigh thee even in thy mouth and in thy heart: that is the word of faith, which we preach.*

So when the word of faith is in our hearts and in our mouths, we speak the word of God by faith, believing that what we say according to God's word will come to pass in Jesus's name, Amen. This is why healing is the children of God's bread; Jesus is this Living bread that dwelt among men and Jesus is our daily bread that we eat when reading the word of God. Jesus is the bread of life and he has given us life abundantly. (Deuteronomy 8:3, John 6:35, Matthew 4:4, Matthew 6:11) In Deuteronomy 8:3 we are told that man doesn't live by bread alone (physical bread) but by every word that proceed out of the mouth.

In John 6:35 we read Jesus saying: *I Am the bread of life: he that comes to me shall never hunger and he that believes on me shall never thirst.* In Matthew 4:4 it is written: *Man shall not live by bread alone but by every word that proceed out of the mouth of God.*

Matthew 6:11 says we are to receive our daily bread. God wants us to be in a place with the foundation of our hearts, Jesus the Christ, studying and reading the word as our daily spiritual meal. When we stay in the word, God will reveal his presence to us in the Spirit as he revealed himself to Moses.

In Exodus 33:18-33, Moses found a place in God; Moses wanted to see God face to face, but no man can see God face to face and live. Moses said to God: *I beseech thee, show me thy glory.* God said to Moses *I will be gracious to whom I will be gracious and will show mercy on whom I will show mercy, thou cannot see my face, for no man see me and live.*

And the Lord said: *Behold there is a place by me and thou shall stand upon a rock (Jesus is the rock in which we shall stand) and it shall come to pass while my glory pass by that I will put thee in the cleft of the rock and I will cover thee with my hand while I pass by and I will take away mine hand and thou shall see my back parts, but my face shall not be seen.*

Jesus even told his disciples: *Have I been so long with you; if you have seen me you have seen the Father for my Father and I are one.* (John 14:8-10) *Phillip said to Jesus Lord show us the Father and it will suffice us. Jesus said to him have I been so long a time with you and yet have thou not known me Phillip? He that has seen me has seen the Father; how say thou then show us the Father? Believe thou not that I Am in the Father, and the Father in me, or else believe me for the very works sake.* When we believe the word of God, Jesus said greater works shall we do because he is with the Father (John 14:12).

When we apply the word of God to our hearts, abide it in the word, live this word, activate this word, which is alive, energizing and penetrates our spiritual hearts to the deepest part of our very nature, our hearts are changed into the heartbeat of God. Meditating on the word of God increases our love, and faith for God and his living, activating, alive word that brings the resuscitating Life of JESUS on the inside of us.

Chapter Twenty-Two

HOW THE WORD WORKS IN OUR SPIRITUAL HEARTS

The seed of God's word is Jesus that is germinated in our spiritual hearts; when we digest this Living Word by applying it daily we are renewed in our hearts and minds for God's purpose.

The seed of God's word is Jesus that empowers us to do God's Kingdom business in the earth realm. We are equipped because of Jesus. We have been granted to do all things through Christ Jesus that strengthens us, growing in the grace and knowledge of Jesus our Lord and Savior. God has given us his divine nature through Jesus Christ, the precious promises that are yes and Amen. When we develop the characteristics and virtues as born-again believers, these are some of the virtues we acquire: faith, knowledge, self-control, perseverance, godliness, brotherly kindness, and the love of God that has been shared in our hearts by the Holy

Spirit. *For the word of God is nigh unto us even in our hearts and in our mouths*, as found in Deuteronomy 30:14.

In the Book of James 1:22 it says for us to be doers of the word and not hearers only deceiving ourselves; we are to be hearers and doers of God's word in order to be in alignment with his will which is his life-giving word. In the book of James, it has a lot to say about the tongue and being unstable. James 1:8 speaks of having a double mind is a person that is unstable in all their ways; whatever we ask God for we must believe, not wavering; it is through our faith in God that we ask in Jesus's name believing we will receive the things we ask according to the word of God. (James 3:5-6)

It is important for us to allow the Lord God to tame our tongues; though our tongues are a little member and boast great things. Our tongues are little but can kindle a great fire and a world of iniquity; our tongues can defile or give life to any given situation or circumstance. God wants to tame our tongues as we surrender our tongues and voices to the power of the Holy Spirit. The Holy Spirit is the teacher, leader, and guide to all truth. Whatever we ask the Father in

Jesus's name when we pray believing God will tame this unruly member in our mouth called the tongue. Life and death is in the power of our tongue. (Proverbs 18:21)

In the book of Romans 4:17 our spiritual Father Abraham called things that be not as though they were; and since the word of God is in our hearts and in our mouths we can call these things to be not as though they were according to the word, and God will perform his word through us. Remember faith comes by hearing, and hearing by the word of God; as we stated these are prescriptions for recovering the spiritual heart.

This is why we must read and study the word of God as our foundation Matthew 6:11 says: *Give us this day our daily bread.* Just as we eat a daily meal to nourish our physical bodies, we have to nourish our spiritual souls and minds to be balanced and healthy spiritually. In Matthew 4:4, it speaks to us again; it is written MAN SHALL NOT LIVE BY BREAD ALONE, BUT BY EVERY WORD THAT PROCEEDS OUT OF THE MOUTH OF GOD (Jesus is speaking in the verse).

As a part of keeping a recovered spiritual heart from a spiritual heart attack we must abide in the word of God that he and Jesus can be one with us and we with them. John 15:4 says: *Abide in me and I in you, as the branch cannot bear fruit of itself except it abide in me.* None of us can bear any type of fruit without abiding in the true vine, which is Jesus. The only way to abide in him is staying in connection with the will of the Father, which is his quick and energizing word that makes us alive in him (Jesus) Amen.

When our spiritual hearts are pure before God, we can see God's glory; this is one of the beatitudes Jesus taught in Matthew 5:8: Blessed is the Kingdom of God.

Happiness produced by the experience of God's favor and especially conditioned by the Revelation of His grace, regardless of their outward condition are the pure in heart, for they shall see God.

When God purifies our hearts through our fiery tests and trials it has a way of giving us a pure heart toward God; and he will allow us to see him in his glory as did Moses.

God's glory can be revealed in our darkest hour if we just focus on all his goodness and mercy toward us.

In Isaiah 60:1-2 (Amplified Version) it says: *Arise from the depression and prostration in which circumstances have kept you- rise to a new life!!! Shine, be radiant with the glory of the Lord has risen upon you. For behold, darkness shall cover the earth, and dense darkness all people, but the Lord shall arise upon (O Jerusalem) and His glory shall be seen on you.*

It is so amazing how much God loves us and will reveal his glory to us. His glory will radiant our continent and we will shine as the light that Jesus has placed in us.

God's Living Word will produce His life and nature in us in this life and we will be able to do all things through Christ Jesus that strengthen us; it is a Supernatural experience in the Realms of the Spirit of God.

When we seek God and his righteousness by choice, asking God to remove any falsehood and unfaithfulness from our hearts, he will do it by our faith. Let's look at what Psalm 119:27-44 says:

Verse 27: make me understand the way of your precepts: so shall I meditate on and talk of your wondrous works.

Verse 28: my life dissolves and weeps (itself away for heaviness); raise me up and strengthen me according to (the promises of) Your word.

Verse 29: remove from me the way of falsehood and unfaithfulness to you and graciously impart your law to me.

Verse 30: I have chosen the way of truth and faithfulness: Your ordinates have I set before me.

Verse 31: I cleave to your testimonies O Lord, put me not to shame.

Verse 32: I will not merely walk, but run the way of your commandments, when you give me a heart that is willing.

Verse 33: teach me, O Lord, the way of your statues, and I will keep it to the very end (steadfastly).

Verse 34: give me understanding, that I may keep your law; yes, I will observe it with my whole heart.

Verse 35: make me go in the path of your commandments, for in them do I delight.

Verse 36: incline my heart to your testimonies and not to (robbery, sensuality, unworthy riches.

Verse 37: turn away my eyes from beholding vanity (idols and idolatry: and restore me to vigorous life and health in your ways.

Verse 38: establish your word and confirm your promise to your servant, which is for those who reverently fear and devotedly worship you.

Verse 39: turn away my reproach which I fear and dread, for your ordinances are good.

Verse 40: behold, I long for your precepts; in your righteousness give me renewed life.

Verse41: let Your mercy and loving-kindness come also me, O Lord, even Your salvation according in Your promise

Verse 42: then, shall I have an answer for those who taunt and reproach me, for I lean on, rely on, and trust in your word.

Verse 43: and take not the word of truth utterly out of my mouth, for I hope in your ordinances.

Verse 44: I will keep your law continually, forever and ever hearing receiving, loving, and obeying it.

Chapter Twenty-Three

CONFESSING GOD'S WORD IS GOOD MEDICATION

When we keep the word of God before our eyes, it enters in our hearts, minds and souls, working healing to our entire beings. It is medicine to our whole heart. As we confess God's word it will transform us into the very image of Jesus. Because of his shed blood, God sees us through the blood without spots, wrinkles or blemishes. We must work to be just like Jesus.

These scriptures will help us to keep a recovery of our spiritual heart by being good medicine for our entire soul, spirit, body and mind. This is why Jesus came to recover man's (humanity) spirit back to the God that created mankind into the image of God the Father, his son Jesus, and the wind of the Spirit to breathe into the lungs of the spirit to make mankind a living spirit and soul. (Genesis 1:26)

If we just think for a moment how excellent the breath of God living on the inside of us is a Supernatural intervention of the God who created the heavens and the earth, it should blow our minds. As we meditate on this awesome experience, confessing and speaking the word should come easier as we lean totally on the promises of God who has great plans for us, Amen. As we realize the plans God has for us are bigger than we can imagine, we should ask God for a Revelation of his knowledge and uncover the truth of who he really is and what he called us to do and be in this earth realm. God wants us not to be dismayed or discouraged; as he told Joshua to be strong and very courageous and not to be dismayed, but to meditate in the word day and night to have good success. (Joshua 1:6-10)

What a plan God had for us! Even before the foundation of the world, God had a backup plan for humanity to be restored from the first spiritual heart attack through receiving Jesus as savior and Lord over our lives and spiritual hearts. Jeremiah 29:11 says: *For I know the thoughts and plans that I have for you says the Lord, thoughts and plans for welfare and peace and not for evil, to give you hope in your final outcome (Amplified Version).*

We must be determined to walk in the word and obey; it requires discipline to walk in obedience to God and his word. It is a profession of our faith and to grow in the grace and knowledge of the Lord Jesus Christ. There is a fight going on and we must fight; we are fighting for our spiritual lives and to keep our hearts in right standing with God. It is a good fight of faith. We have to be strong in the Lord Jesus and in the power of his might; we have to learn how to dwell in the secret place of the Most High God, allowing him to reside continuously in our hearts through an intimate fellowship in the word and in prayer, with the whole armor of God on as his heavenly representatives and mighty army on this earth. No foe can stand against the power of almighty God, Amen.

When we dwell in the secret place of the Most High God, it will allow us to be inaccessible to our enemy and his demons. This doesn't mean he won't be on the prowl seeking whom he can devour. We are to resist him in the Lord and give him no place. We have to remember to keep on the full amour: the helmet of salvation, the breastplate of righteousness, our loins girdle about with truth, the shield of faith, the sword of the spirit which is the word of God, our feet shod with the preparation of the gospel of peace. There are two other weapons we never speak of; they are the weapons of worship and prayer.

The weapon of praise and worship releases the anointing of God that destroys yokes and will undo heavy burdens. It does not only break chains, but will destroy the chains that bind us, and we have been given the power of the Holy Spirit to conquer and overcome our enemies, and it is through worship, praise and the living word. As God has given us the healing balm of the Spirit of Jesus by empowering us to victory, learning how to use the weapons of our warfare, which isn't carnal but might through God to the pulling down of strongholds in the name of Jesus (2 Corinthians 10:4). These weapons are used to cast down imaginations and every high thing that would exalt itself against the knowledge of God.

When our enemy comes against our hearts and minds, against the promises of God for our lives, we must take the authority we've been given along with the word of God and command the word to work for us by speaking the word by faith and watch Jesus create the answer, Amen.

It is imperative to work the word of God to pull down the works of the kingdom of darkness; it is a part of keeping our spiritual hearts healthy, enlarges our faith, helps to keep our spiritual hearts recovered from any spiritual heart ailment, or conditions us to exercise our spiritual heart muscles in Jesus's name, hallelujah. The word in us is Jesus the living bread, which leads to his abundance of life and the greater life shines in us and through us to enlighten our eyes and mind of understanding.

When Jesus walked the face of this earth, he walked in the Supernatural Realm by teaching his disciples how to live and speak of his Kingdom; to believe in the word that he spoke things to as they were and they became a reality of his faith. When we learn by Jesus's example how powerful his word is, we will see miracles, sign, and wonders as a lifestyle. Let me explain what I mean. In the book of Genesis, the first chapter, verses 1-3: *In the beginning God created the heaven and the earth. And the earth was without form and void and darkness was upon the face of the deep and the Spirit of God moved upon the face of the waters. And God said, let there be light and there was light.*

If we ask God for the Revelation of creation and how Jesus was with him in the beginning, and what part Jesus had in creation, it took the Father just to speak the word that is Jesus, who created the heaven and the earth. As we study this book and verses, look at what the Holy Spirit revealed through Revelation. God spoke light. Jesus, being the living word, was what created the heaven and the earth. God was speaking the word. Jesus created the light because he is Light. God was speaking: Jesus, go create the light.

In Hebrews 4:12 the Amplified Version says: *The word God speaks is alive and full of power (making it active) operative, energizing, and effective; it is sharper than any two-edged sword, penetrating to the dividing line of the breath of life (soul) and the immortal spirit.*

The word that God speaks gives life. Jesus being the life gave life to the stars, moon, and sun. All that is on the earth Jesus gave life to, because he is the Spirit of life and through him we were given life through the shedding of his blood and confessing with our mouths, receiving him in our hearts. Amen.

In reading Proverbs 8:6-13, we will learn an example of the word God speaks, how excellent things proceed out of his mouth, only truth is uttered and full of righteousness. With God there is truth and righteousness, nothing contrary to his own words. God's word makes all crooked pathways and things straight.

In the book of Proverbs 8:6-13 and Proverbs 6:15-30 (Amplified Version) it says: *Hear, for I will speak excellent and princely things; and the opening of my lips shall be right things.*

Verse 7: For my mouth shall utter truth, and wrongdoing is detestable and loathsome to my lips.

Verse 8: All the words of my mouth are righteous (upright and in right standing) with God there is nothing contrary to truth or crooked in them.

Verse 9: They are all plain to him who understands (and opens his heart), and right to those who find knowledge and live by it.

Verse 10: Receive my instruction in preference to (striving for) silver, and knowledge rather than choice gold.

Verse 11: For skillful and godly wisdom is better than rubies or pearls, and all things that may be desired are not to be compared to it.

Verse 12: I, wisdom (from God), make prudence my dwelling, and I find out knowledge and discretion.

Verse 13: The reverent fear and worshipful awe of the Lord (includes) the hatred of evil: pride, arrogance, the evil way, and perverted and twisted speech I hate.

When God was speaking, he was speaking Jesus. The power of God is Jesus, the Living word that became flesh. So Jesus is the creative power of God. Ephesians 3:9 says: *And to make all men see what is the fellowship of the mystery; which from the beginning of the world hath been hid in God who created all things by Jesus Christ.*

Let's continue to see this truth in Proverbs 8:14-30 which speaks as this:

Verse 14: I have counsel and sound knowledge, I have understanding, I have might and power.

Verse 15: by me kings reign and rulers decree justice (reference Dan. 2:21 and Rom. 13:1).

Verse 16: by me princes' rule. And nobles even all the judges and governors of the earth.

Verse 17: I love those who love me, and those who seek me early and diligently shall find me (reference 1 Sam. 2:30, Ps. 91:14, John 14:21 and James 1:5).

Verse 18: Riches and honor are with me, enduring wealth and righteousness in every area and relation, and right standing with God. (Reference Prov. 3:16 and Matt. 6:33).

Verse 19: My fruit is better than gold, yes than refined gold and my increase than choice silver.

Verse 20: I (Wisdom) walk in the way of righteousness (moral and spiritual rectitude in every area of relation); in the midst of the paths of justice.

Verse 21: that I may cause those who love me to inherit (true) riches and that I may fill their treasuries.

Verse 22: The Lord formed and brought me (Wisdom) forth at the beginning of His way, before His acts of old.

Verse 23: I (Wisdom) was inaugurated and ordained from everlasting from the beginning, before ever the earth existed (Reference John 1:1 and 1 Cor. 1:24).

Verse 24: when there were no deep, I was brought forth, when there were no fountains laden with water.

Verse 25: before the mountains were settled before the hills, I was brought forth (reference Job 15: 7-8).

Verse 26: while as yet He had not made the land or the fields or the first of the dust of the earth.

Verse 27: when He prepared the heavens I (Wisdom) was there: when He drew a circle upon the face of the deep and stretched out the firmament over it.

Verse 28: when he made the firm the sky above, when he established fountains of the deep.

Verse 29: when He gave to the sea it's (limit and His decree that the waters should not transgress (across the boundaries set by His command, when He appointed the foundations of the earth (Job 38:10-11, Ps. 104:6-9. Jer. 5:22).

Verse 30: Then I Wisdom was beside Him as a master and director of the work; and I was daily His delight, rejoicing before Him always.

As we receive the Revelation, God is revealing the mystery of who Jesus really is and this Great Power is abiding in us. This mighty word which is Jesus is the name that is above every name; and as we learn how powerful this Living Bread is within us, the word in our hearts and in our mouths is so powerful that when we speak it, according to God has placed it in our hearts, it brings life to every situation, circumstance, and problem that will occur in this life. The word is anointed to destroy yokes and bondages, even the power of darkness. The Anointing is of God and not of us; each of us are given the anointing for whatever work God has called us to do.

Chapter Twenty-Four

GOD HAS CALLED EACH OF US FOR HIS PURPOSE

What has God called you to do in the Kingdom? Whatever it is, you are anointed to do the will of God and as Jesus spoke: *not my will but thou will be done.* We must speak the word as the Father commands through the power of the Holy Spirit. It is in the word in 2 Corinthians 4:1-4 *Therefore seeing we have this ministry; as we received mercy we faint not. But have renounced the hidden things of dishonesty, not handling the word of God deceitfully; but manifestation of the truth commenting ourselves to every man's conscience in the sight of God. But if our gospel be hid it is hid to them that are lost. In whom the god of this world hath blinded the minds of them which believe not, lest the light of the glorious gospel of Christ Jesus, who is the image of God, should shine unto them.*

God wants us as sold-out believers to stop handling his word deceitfully and be not only hearers of his word, but doers of the word of God. Many people are dying and going to hell because we have been hypocritical; we speak to our brothers and sisters from our lips that we love them; but in our hearts we lie, we gossip about one another, we have become busybodies, faultfinders, going from phone line to phone line, minding other people's business, and the world is looking, seeing, hearing how we treat one another and wants no part of this salvation.

Some of us have stopped seeking the Kingdom of God. We are seeking the kingdoms of the world. God is calling us back to intercession, crying out to God for real; we need to remember we once was lost and God found us and we need to repent. All of this is a part of the Recovery of our SPIRITUAL HEART FROM A SPIRITUAL HEART ATTACK.

Remembering God is a Spirit and he deals with our spirits, God is love and this love was shared abroad in our hearts by the Holy Spirit. We must guard our hearts with all diligence, for out of the abundance of our hearts our mouths speak.

Whatever is in our hearts the most, will proceed out of our mouths. If the word of God is in our hearts the most, the word of God will proceed out of our mouths. This is why it is so important to speak the word of God only. As we continue in 2 Corinthians 4:5: *for we preach not ourselves but Christ Jesus the Lord: and ourselves your servants for Jesus' sake.*

Verse 6: *It was God who commanded the light to shine out of darkness; hath shined in our hearts, to give the light of the knowledge of the glory of God in the face of Jesus Christ.* When we came into the Kingdom of God he gives the knowledge of the glory of God in the face of Jesus Christ, who has shined in our hearts when we allowed him to come into our hearts.

Verse 7: *But we have this treasure in earthen vessels, which the Excellency of the power may be of God and not of us.* Hallelujah, in these earthen vessels there is such an Excellency of the power of God in us through Jesus and the Holy Spirit because of the Revelation, Knowledge, and Truth, that only the teacher, the Holy Spirit, uncovers and reveals the Mystery of His Kingdom.

It is through my spiritual journey within the last thirteen-and-a-half years, that God has been and is teaching me how to recover from my spiritual heart attack. I had to take a look at my spiritual heart, confess with my mouth the things that church folk had done knowingly or unknowingly, and to forgive them that I could totally be free. Some were even pastors who may have misunderstood me; they may or may not have had a personal relationship with God themselves. I remember reading this book by John Osteen years ago, *The Confessions of a Baptist Preacher*. In this book he admitted not knowing the God he was preaching about until he accepted Jesus and was baptized in the Holy Spirit. Many of us have been called out of our darkness; few have been chosen to teach and preach the gospel. Many have their own agendas and are building their own kingdom and think it is all about themselves and no more. Remember the power is of God and we have this ministry in these vessels of clay, Christ Jesus in us, the hope of glory. Amen.

I've learned and still am learning it is not about their agendas or my having my own agenda; it is about God's Kingdom Agenda and the assignments he gives us to complete. Jesus had an awesome assignment given to him by his Father. As the Father commanded to come into this sinful world to save humanity because God loves the creatures he created after his image and likeness and wishes no soul to be lost, but all would accept his forgiveness through his son Jesus by receiving and accepting him in their hearts.

God wants to receive the lost souls from their spiritual heart attacks so he can recover them from sin and they too can gain eternal life in Jesus Christ. It takes a step of faith because eternal life is a gift from God and those who believe; as many as call on the Lord Jesus Christ shall be saved, and they shall become sons of God. Salvation is not of our works that we boast, it is a gift from God. This is how much his love is for us. Amen

I want Jesus to be enthroned in my heart and not me being enthroned in myself, but wrapped up, overflowing in the power of his might, made strong in him, steadfast, unmovable, always abounding in the work of the Lord Jesus Christ, giving his Father and mine all the glory due his name, Amen.

I forgive all those who rejected me, hurt me, misunderstood me, came in my life with hidden agendas, took my kindness for a weakness, misused me, lied on me, and tried to deceive me. I now know what the devil tried to do; he was trying to get me off my God-given assignment for God's glory and to be one of many that would pray for the lost souls and that the Body of Believers would come into the unity of our faith. Walking in the Love of God in Christ Jesus without hidden agendas, being as the Father and the son are one, as members of Jesus's body can be one with the Father and the son, and one with one another in Jesus's name, Amen.

God called me out of the devil's dark kingdom into his son Jesus's Kingdom of light in 1977 to preach, teach the word of God, to teach effectiveness of having an intimate relationship with him, to training others what intercession was in my home church of Beulah Baptist Church where I organized an intercessory prayer group. God gave me three different books of the Old Testament to read: Isaiah, Jeremiah, and Ezekiel. When I read Jeremiah 1:5 is when I realized God had chosen me to proclaim the gospel before I entered my mother's womb. I ran from preaching the gospel because I wanted to be real and not play with God; now I know my spiritual arms are too short to box with God. I am totally surrendered and sold out to him as I have read in Isaiah 61:1-11. When God calls us out of darkness and into the light of his son Jesus's Kingdom to do the work of his Kingdom, we must obey to be prosperous. God spoke to me that I was his messenger and that he had placed his word in my mouth to speak it and to draw not back so I can live naturally and spiritually healthy. God has revealed many things to me in the Spirit Realm. I am learning when and how to release them in his correct timing.

I have had visions of God sitting in his throne room, writing in the Lamb's Book of life, but I never saw his face. I was standing behind him and asked "who are you?" He spoke and said to me "you know who I am." Through my experience from a child until now I really didn't understand. There are still things that come to me and God gives me Revelations and interpretations. There is nothing as wonderful as spending time with God in his word and prayer. God is calling all believers to get in alignment with his divine will and purpose for our lives, to let him wash us whiter than snow. God is calling the body of Jesus Christ to order, to come up in the Spirit Realm and to fight the good fight of faith, to hear him and to obey him. There is a sound God is listening for from us; it is a sound of unity and one accord. Come on, Zion, rise up into our rightful place in God and stand still to see the Salvation of our God. These are the days of Elijah, Paul, John, Peter, James. All miracles and signs and wonders are happening in heaven and on this earth. Get ready and stay, be ready when Jesus comes. Amen.

We have this treasure in earthen vessels that the Power and Light of Jesus might shine into the darkness of this world and radiate throughout the world by coming into the knowledge of God's truth to witness to the Light within us, to shine among mankind, that may see our good works and give glory to God, Amen.

We have been given the comforter, the intercessor, the advocate, strengthener, counselor, the standby, the helper, the leader, and the guide that guides us into the whole truth. This was the promise Jesus made to his disciples and it is still true today. It is not that we have to rehearse what we will speak, for the Holy Spirit will be the one doing the speaking through these vessels of clay, according to John 16:13-15: *Howbeit when the Spirit of truth is come, he will guide you into all truth; for he shall not speak of himself, but only what the Father speaks to him will he reveal it to us.* God has given us his plan and as long as we stick with the plan, we will be successful. (Study Jeremiah 29: 11-12)

Chapter Twenty-Five

THE SPIRITUAL HEART AND THE POWER IN PRAYER

As we learn the power of intercessory prayer and how God wants an intimate relationship with his children, we will come to realize this is one of the many tools to recover our spiritual hearts, to be stable and inseparable to the scalpel of the word by cutting away the foreskin of sin and unrighteousness. Psalm 5:1-3 says: *Listen to my words, O Lord, give heed to my sighing and groanings: hear my voice O Lord in the morning I prepare a prayer, a sacrifice for you and watch and wait for you to speak to my heart.*

As we are still to hear the Spirit of God speaking and have an open ear to hear what the Spirit of God is saying and obey, God is speaking. Are we taking the time to be still and listen? We must stand still and be still to hear him speaking. God will give strength to the weak and the faint in heart. Isaiah 40:29-31 says: *He (God) gives power to the faint; and to them that have no might he increase strength. Even the youth shall faint and be weary, and the young men shall utterly fall. But they that wait upon the Lord shall renew their strength; they shall mount up with wings of eagles, they shall run and not be weary and they shall walk and not faint.* Amen

In Daniel 9:3-4 we find Daniel interceding for himself and Israel; it reads as thus: *And I (Daniel) set my face unto the Lord God to seek by prayer and supplications with fasting and sackcloth, and ashes. And I (Daniel) prayed unto the Lord my God and made my confession and, O Lord the great and dreadful God, keeping the covenant and mercy to them that love him and to them that keep his commandments.*

God has given us the heavenly Kingdom's strategies to overcome and to be more than conquerors through renewing our strength in the word, the prayer of intercession, and the faith of God to conquer our enemy, the devil, against his plots, schemes, hindrances, blockages, tricks, dark strategies of rulers of the darkness of this world, principalities, powers, and plans of the devil's kingdom in Jesus's name, Amen.

God has given us defensive weaponry of his Supernatural Kingdom to fight the good fight of faith, doing all to stand in Jesus's liberty. We must know the weapons of our warfare and be skillful in using them. We have been violently attacked by the devil and his demonic army, and it is imperative that we take it back by force, through the word of God and the Holy Spirit in Jesus's name, Amen. (Matthew 11:12)

Take back our spiritual sanctuaries, our lives, our communities, our schools, our prayer lives and houses, take back our marriages, take back our sons and daughters, and take back our government, our states and this whole country, the world for the Kingdom of our God.

God is calling us to wake up Zion out of our slumber and sleeping in these dangerous times that are so very evil. We don't have to fear. God has not given us a spirit of fear, but love, power, and a sound mind. (2 Timothy 1:7)

God is calling us to realignment with his Kingdom's principals, to walk up right before him, and to come to his Kingdom's order, not to break our ranks, and to come into total unity with himself and with one another. We must focus on building the Kingdom of God by ushering in souls for the Kingdom and going out into the hedges, highways, and byways, telling a dying generation about a savior that can do the impossible and change a generation to meet the soon coming King of kings and Lord of lords.

We must be ignited again and set ablaze with the Power of the Holy Spirit. We need to seek the face and will of God, call an all-night prayer meeting without our own agendas, but allow the Holy Spirit to orchestrate the Kingdom Agenda and let salvation, deliverance, worship, and healing take place that the Shekinah Glory of God will take over the meeting and the fire of God consume the very foreskin our hearts. As Abraham sacrificed the lamb instead of Isaac, we need to lay ourselves on the altar of sacrifice, allowing the Holy Spirit to take full control. We need to lay our lives down as a sacrificial offering to God by sailing out and surrendering our very lives for our King and his Kingdom.

Call me crazy, but am I hearing from God? Who are you hearing from? The trumpet of God is sounding for a gathering of the members of the body of his son Jesus to come to order; God is restoring all that the cankerworm, the palmerworm, the locust, and the caterpillar has eaten up; our true praise and worship, our prayer life, our love for one another, our heart of compassion, our love for God and one another. (Joel 1:4)

Some of us are drunken by the many things of this world and not about the Kingdom of God. Prayer truly will change things and it all starts with our coming back to the very things that brought us out of darkness by restoring our lives back to God's Kingdom. Tell someone about Jesus and all he has done and is doing for us. It's not about the stuff we obtain, it is about his will. God will bless us materially, but the cart cannot go before the horse; we must not make these things our idols.

Jesus should be our first priority, seeking first the Kingdom of God and all his righteousness, and he will add these other things. 3 John 1:2 says: *Beloved, I wish above all things that thou may prosper and be in health even as thy soul prospers. God want the whole entire spirit, soul body and mind to prosper including the material Amen.*

As believers, Joel 1:5 is calling us to *awake you drunkards, and weep and howl all you drinkers of wine, because of the new wine (the Holy Spirit) for it is cut off from your mouth.*

We must drink into the Spirit in order to be filled. Too many of us want to drink and be refreshed in the Spirit of God; let the power of God empower us to the overflowing power until all we want is Jesus in the morning, Jesus in the evening, Jesus when we lay down to sleep, so we can change our communities, homes, our marriages, our schools, colleges, the jail systems, and our families. When these situations are changed, the prayer houses will change.

James 5:17-18 says: *Elias was a praying man subject to like passions as we are and he prayed earnestly that it might not rain: and it rained not on the earth by the space of three years and six months. And he prayed again and the heaven gave rain and the earth brought forth her fruit.* Now do we see how one man full of faith in God and the power to believe and trust the word he spoke? Now if this man had that kind of power and faith, Jesus had not come to the earth yet. Since Jesus has come, we have been empowered to do greater works, but we are living beneath our heavenly privileges. We need to come up in the Spirit Realm and hear and see what the Spirit of God is saying to the churches.

When you read these pages of this book, hear God speaking to your spiritual heart; God needs a broken and contrite spiritual heart that he can trust with his Kingdom keys to utilize the keys to the treasury of heaven, calling those things to be not as they were, achieving Kingdom Power to bring heaven down to earth. The portal of the Third heaven is open and the angels are releasing Kingdom strategies for us to overcome the powers of darkness.

The Spirit of God is speaking; recover your spiritual heart. It is an individual assignment. Trust the Holy Spirit; he is speaking to my spirit and using my fingers to type out these pages. It is a Supernatural experience I am having just listening to the Spirit of God flowing into my very spiritual heart. As you read these words straight from the throne of heaven, give attention to what the Spirit of God is saying to you individually and corporately. The churches need to hear what the Spirit of God is saying. Come together; it is time out for being a divided body of believers. Be unified in the name of Jesus.

Remember, Jesus is the examining Physician who specializes in things that are impossible and he can do what no other power can do. Let Jesus resuscitate your spiritual heart back to his life. God is waiting to breathe in us, on us, and through us to empower us for his plan and purpose. Won't you let him renew and restore you to enter the garden of your heart? May he give you a fresh start and new beginnings; there is so much power in the name of Jesus and in the blood of Jesus. I am not the same even as my fingers touch these keys on the keyboard; my spiritual heart was wounded and now there is such a release and a relief. The power of the Holy Spirit is so strong on me, in me, my spirit man is overjoyed. I never felt like this before and on another plane, there is such a shifting occurring in my spirit.

We can all experience this wonderful change as God is waiting to refresh our spirit man and revive us again. The spiritual rain cloud is gathering to pour out a greater anointing for the end time harvest of souls; God wants our hearts to be prepared for this great assignment. Get ready and stay ready.

The glory cloud is rising and the latter-day rain is falling. We must open our spiritual hearts up to the Living God as his Living word will produce his life and nature in us in this life, and we can be seated in heavenly places with Christ Jesus far above all principality, and power, and might, and dominion, and every name that is named, not only in this world but also in that which is to come. (Ephesians 1:21) We are also made to sit in heavenly places with Christ Jesus. (Ephesians 2:6) And God has raised us up together in heavenly places in Christ Jesus.

In Ephesians, the Apostle Paul gives us an example of how powerful prayer and Revelation can be in our lives to help us keep a recovered spiritual heart. The Apostle Paul is speaking of the revelation of the mystery of The Church. He starts his prayer like this: (Ephesians 1:15)

Verse 15: Wherefore I also, after I heard of your faith in the Lord Jesus and love unto all the saints.

Verse 16: Cease not to give thanks for you, making mention of you in my prayers.

Verse 17: that the God of our Lord Jesus Christ; the Father of glory, may give unto you the spirit of wisdom and revelation in the knowledge of him.

Verse 18: The eyes of your understanding being enlightened, that you may know what the hope of his calling is, and what the riches of the glory of his inheritance in the saints.

Verse 19: And what is the exceeding greatness of his power to us-ward who believes, according to the working of his mighty power.

Verse 20: Which he wrought in Christ, when he raised him from the dead; and set him at his own right hand in heavenly places.

Verse 21: Far above all principality, and power and might. and dominion, and every name that is named, not only in this world, but also in that which to come.

Verse 22: And hath put all things under his feet and gave him to be the head over all things the church.

Verse 23: Which is his body the fullness of him that fill all in all.

God wants us to have the spirit of wisdom and revelation of the knowledge of him; our eyes of understanding to be enlightened, that we may know the hope of our calling and what the riches of the glory of the inheritance of the saints.

We need to know the exceeding greatness of the power of God in us, through Jesus Christ. When he was raised up from the dead, this same resurrected power that raised Jesus from the dead is within us; we need to know how to use it.

Ephesians 2:4-9 says: *But God who is rich in mercy, for his great love wherewith he loved us. Even when we were dead in sins, hath quicken us together with Christ, by grace are you saved. And hath raised us up together and made us sit together in heavenly places in Christ Jesus. That in the ages to come he might show the exceeding riches of his grace in his kindness toward us through Christ Jesus. For by grace are you saved through faith: and not of yourselves, it is the gift of God. Not of works, lest any man should boast.*

God is so merciful, rich in his grace and great love toward us, you have been quickened together with Jesus Christ even when we were dead in our sins. God has raised us together with Jesus Christ and made us to sit together in heavenly places, that he might show his exceeding riches of his grace in his kindness to us through Jesus Christ our Lord. It is not because of anything we have done that we should boast, it is through the gift of God we are saved. We have nothing to boast but the goodness and mercy of God. We should remember God's goodness, love, and mercy toward and Selah about it (meaning to calmly think over it).

We need to stop grieving the Holy Spirit by our agendas and programs. It is all about the Kingdom of God and building his Kingdom up by witnessing to the lost, destitute, feeble in body and mind, the hungry, the lonely, the sick and shut-ins, the homeless, the widows, and those that are in the body who are hurting and in pain mentally and spiritually.

We need to have a compassionate heart of recovery to get back the heartbeat of God, to be sensitive to others. Ask the Holy Spirit to search our hearts and take inventory of why we have some spiritual heart ailments and heart conditions. God is calling us to seek him like never before. This is a real time to die to self and let Jesus resuscitate us by breathing the fresh wind of the Holy Spirit in our spirit man now in Jesus's name, Amen.

It is very important to have an intimate relationship with God through the power of prayer and his word. We have to have quality time in fellowship with our creator to keep our spiritual hearts in a recovery mode. Remember, God is a Spirit and we must get in the Spirit to nourish our spirit man. Jesus is our example of how he spent time in prayer with his Father to hear the direction and instruction as he walked the face of this earth. Remember when Jesus spoke, he always spoke of the words he heard his Father speak to him in prayer. He would be alone by going to a quiet place to communicate with the Father in prayer.

Now think about what you just read. Ask God to help you to receive this revelation of this very statement; if it took

Jesus time in prayer to get direction and instruction from the Father, what do you think we have to do? We must take the time to spend in prayer to get an intimate relationship, get direction, instruction and clarity of what to do, what to say, how to bring it to pass, through the power of the Holy Spirit, how to hear from the Father and obey what is being said for us to do.

Remember, it is not our words but it is the word of the Holy Spirit speaking to us what the Father is instructing the Holy Spirit to give us to do. The conversation the Father and the Holy Spirit has as the Holy Spirit relays God's message to us is found in John 16:13: *Howbeit when the Spirit of Truth is come , he will guide you into all truth for he shall not speak of himself but whatsoever he shall hear, that shall he speak and he will show you things to come.*

John 15: 26 says: *But when the Comforter is come, whom I will send unto you from the Father, even the Spirit of truth, which proceeds from the Father he shall testify of me.*

When we are in prayer, allow the Holy Spirit to speak to our hearts. Ask the Lord God to open up our spiritual ears to hear what the Spirit is speaking to our spirit man. We must have an anointed ear to hear God's voice. The word of God says to us: *he that has an ear hear what the spirit (God) is saying to the churches.* Revelation 2:7 says: *He that hath an ear let him hear what the Spirit said unto the churches, to him that overcometh will I give to eat of the tree life which is in the midst of the paradise of God.*

As we see, it states in this word, an ear to hear, not ears to hear. It means to have a spiritual ear to hear from the Holy Spirit. Let us notice the word "heart" and see how there are three different words found here: hear, ear, and art. So the spiritual ear must hear what the spirit of God is speaking and it takes an art to be skillful in hearing the voice of God and what he is speaking. Our spiritual ear must be sensitive to hear the Holy Spirit of God and be willing to obey.

Our prayers are a communication line to God's heavenly throne; it is a two-way conversation to what the spirit of God will speak as we listen attentively for directions, and instructions on his Kingdom Agenda. God will give each of us a Kingdom assignment to complete as we follow the leading of the Holy Spirit, Amen.

We must ask God for his wisdom, knowledge, and understanding, and how to use them. In Daniel 1:17 it says: *As for these four children, God gave them knowledge and skill in all learning and wisdom and Daniel had understanding in all visions and dreams.*

We must see that God will give us what we ask in faith, believing according to his word. His word is very real. My children have stood on this very scripture and I have given it to many other parents whose children were having difficulties in their school work. It works.

At the age of 63, I graduated from college, standing on this very scripture and it does work alone with all the promises in the word of God. Every promise in the word of God will prosper in the things that we believe, trust in, and work. The word does and will work for our good.

God will uncover and reveal his secrets of his word to us as we spend time in prayer and studying his holy word. It will transform us into the very image of his son Jesus. We can gain insight and revelation knowledge and revelation truth. There is nothing like the wisdom of God which is easily to be entreated, and first of all peaceful. It is not infallible, puffed-up, haughty but humble and meek. The word will give us the strength we need in every situation, every circumstance, every challenge we face and how to overcome, Amen.

God will keep us in his perfect peace as we keep our minds stayed on him. (Isaiah 26:3)

These words and scripture can keep our spiritual heart in the recovery mode if we believe and stand, nothing wavering, confess the word, and knowing God will keep our spirit, soul, body and mind.

As we look at Job 22:21-30, reacquainting ourselves to God is the way to keep us recovering from a Spiritual Heart Attack and any other spiritual heart conditions. Job 22: 21-30 says:

Verse 21: Acquaint now thyself with him (God) and be at peace: thereby good shall come unto thee:

Verse 22: Receive, I pray thee, the law from his mouth, and lay up his words in thine heart.

Verse 23: If thou return to the Almighty, thou shall be built up, thou shall put away iniquity far from thy tabernacles.

Verse 24: Then shall thou layup gold as dust and the gold of Ophir as the stones of the brooks.

Verse 25: Yea, the Almighty shall be thy defense, and thou shall have plenty of silver.

Verse 26: For then shall thou have thy delight in the Almighty and shall lift up thou face unto God.

Verse 27: Thou shall make thy prayer unto him and he shall hear thee and thou shall pay thy vows.

Verse 28: Thou shall also decree a thing and it shall be established unto thee and thy light shall shine upon thy ways.

Verse 29: When men are cast down, then thou shall say there is a lifting up and he shall save the humble person.

Verse 30: He shall deliver the island of the innocent and it is delivered by the pureness of thine hands. Amen.

As we speak forth God's word, we can decree and declare his words to create answers to pray in Jesus's name. Jesus will us give answers to our prayers as we pray in his name. In order to receive, we must believe and be forgiving, that we can receive the blessings of the Lord God in Jesus's name, Amen.

As we can see, the word in our hearts and mouths will bring great things into our lives through prayer, by speaking the word of God into the atmosphere. As we confess, decree, and declare, the word of God will change our entire lives as we believe in Jesus's name, Amen.

We can enjoy living with peace, goodness, grace, and the mercy of God when we stand to be corrected, instructed, and guided by the word and the power of the Holy Spirit.

As this book is for the healing of a Spiritual Heart Attack and the Spiritual heart ailments that can occur during our spiritual journey, these verses of scriptures can be a prescription medication to healing our spiritual hearts as the Great Physician prescribes directions for our healing. As we study what occurs in the spiritual heart and read and pray, the word of God through the power of the Holy Spirit will assist us in understanding the importance of giving God our whole heart (spirit).

We must remember God's word will never return to him void, it will accomplish just what he sends it to do. The word of God must be in our hearts and in our mouths, and we must speak it forth in order for him to watch over it to perform it, and it will come to pass in Jesus's name, Amen.

Chapter Twenty-Six

THE SPIRITUAL HEART HEARS BY THE WORD OF GOD

Remember, faith does come by hearing the word of God; as the word of God is heard, faith comes. As we seek God in our prayers, we need to know what words to stand to plead our causes; this is a way to get the word of God into our hearts as we speak and read the word aloud.

We need to always think on the goodness of God and what he has done, and what he is going to do, for this spiritual walk is a continuous journey daily.

Let's look at the power of praise and worship in keeping a spiritual heart recovered. Psalm 34:1-19 says:

Verse 1: I will bless the Lord at all times: his praise shall continually be in my mouth.

Verse 2: My soul shall make her boast in the Lord, the humble shall hear thereof and be glad.

Verse 3: O magnify the Lord with me and let us exalt his name together.

Verse 4: I sought the Lord, and he heard me, and delivered me from all my fears.

Verse 5: They looked unto him, and were lightened, and their faces were not ashamed.

Verse 6: This poor man cried, and the Lord heard him, and saved him out of all his troubles.

Verse 7: The angels of the Lord encamp round and about them that fear him and deliver them.

Verse 8: O taste and see that the Lord is good: blessed is the man that trust in him.

Verse 9: O fear the Lord, you his saints for there is no want to them that fear him.

Verse 10: The young lion do lack, and suffer hunger but they that seek the Lord shall not want any good thing.

Verse 11: Come ye children, hearken unto me, I will teach you the fear of the Lord.

Verse 12: What man is he that desires life and love many days that he may see good?

Verse 13: Keep thy tongue from evil and thy lips from speaking guile.

Verse 14: Depart from evil and do good, seek peace and pursue it.

Verse 15: The eyes of the Lord are upon the righteous, and his ears are open unto their cry.

Verse 16: The face of the Lord is against them that do evil, to cut off the remembrance of them from the earth.

Verse 17: The righteous cry and the Lord hear and deliver them out of all their troubles.

Verse 18: The Lord is nigh them unto them that are of a broken heart and save such as be of a contrite spirit.

Verse 19: Many are the afflictions of the righteous, but the Lord delivers him out of them all.

The last verse of Psalm 34:19 allows us to know that there are many afflictions of the righteous; we have to allow the Spirit of God to restore our spiritual hearts to oneness with the Father and his son Jesus. Afflictions will come into each of our lives. We must know how to work the word of God, for it is our deliverance in every situation, circumstance, problem, or heart alignment. As we study God's word, the Holy Spirit will bring different scriptures to our remembrance that we can use to be victorious in all things.

We need the grace and peace of God to be multiplied unto us through the knowledge of God and of Jesus Christ. In the book of 2 Peter 1:2-21, the apostle Peter writes to the church of how to grow in Christ Jesus. This is a lesson that will not grow old for us as believers in Jesus Christ. As we study these verses, let the Holy Spirit minister to your hearts.

In 2 Peter 1:2-21, Verse 2 says: *Grace and peace be multiplied unto you through the knowledge of God, and of Jesus Christ.* It takes our knowing our God through knowledge of Jesus, who is the living word that became flesh. God is a Spirit and we are recreated in our spirit man after the image of God the Father, the son Jesus, and the Holy Spirit as teacher, leader, guide, intercessor, advocate, strengthener, and standby. The Holy Spirit will help us to rightly divide the word of God in truth, for he is the Spirit of Truth.

2 Peter 1:3 reads as thus: *According as his divine power hath given unto us all things that pertain to life and godliness, through the knowledge of him that hath called us to glory and virtue.* We have been called according to God's divine power and nature, unto all things that pertain to life and godliness through the knowledge of God through Jesus Christ.

It should be a part of our will to come into the knowledge of who God is and to get to know him in an intimate relationship, through his word and prayer.

2 Peter 1:4: *Whereby are given unto us exceeding great and precious promises, that by these ye might be partakers of the divine nature, having escaped the corruption that is in the world through lust.*

Verse 5: And beside this giving all diligence, add to your faith, virtue and to virtue knowledge:

Verse 6: And to knowledge temperance, and to temperance patience, and to patience godliness.

Verse 7: And to godliness, brotherly kindness and to brotherly kindness charity.

Verse 8: For if these things, be in you and abound, they make you that you neither be barren nor unfruitful in the knowledge of our Lord Jesus Christ.

Verse 9: But he that lack these things is blind and cannot see afar off, and hath forgotten that he was purged from his old sins.

Verse 10: Wherefore the rather, brethren give diligence to make your calling and election sure for if you do these things, you shall never fall.

Verse 11: For so an entrance shall be ministered unto you abundantly unto the everlasting kingdom of our Lord and Savior Jesus Christ.

Verse 12: Wherefore I will not be negligent to put you always in remembrance of these things, though you know them and be established in the present truth.

Verse 13: Yea, I think it meet as long, as I am in this tabernacle to stir you up by putting you in remembrance.

Verse 14: Knowing that shortly I must put off this tabernacle, even as our Lord Jesus Christ hath showed me.

Verse 15: Moreover I will endeavor that you may be able after my decrease to have these things always in remembrance.

Verse 16: For we have not followed cunningly devised fables; when we made known unto you the power and coming of our Lord Jesus Christ but were eyewitnesses of his majesty.

Verse 17: For he received from God the Father honor and glory, when there came such a voice to him from the excellent glory, this is my beloved son in whom I am well pleased.

Verse 18: And the voice, which came from heaven, we heard when we were with him in the holy mount.

Verse 19: We have also a more sure word of prophecy, whereunto you do well that you take heed, as unto a light that shines in a dark place, until the day dawn, and the day star arise in your hearts.

Verse 20: Knowing this first that no prophecy of the scripture is of any private interpretation.

Verse 21: For the prophecy came not in old times by the will of man, but holy men of God spoke as they were moved by the Holy Ghost.

This reading of Apostle Peter is for our learning and instruction to get the word of God deep down into our spirits (hearts) and study them in order to grow up spiritually in the Lord Jesus Christ, Amen.

We have to learn that the Lord is our rock and our salvation; he is the rock on which we stand.

Knowing this is the foundation of our faith, who is Jesus, let's look at Psalm 62:1-2 and then Psalm 62:5-8.

Psalm 62: 1-2 says: *Truly my soul wait upon God: from him comes my salvation. He only is my rock and my salvation he is my defense, I shall not be greatly moved.*

Psalm 62: 5-8 says: *My soul wait thou only upon God, for my expectation is from him. He only is my rock and my salvation, he is my defense, I shall not be moved. In God is my salvation and my glory, the rock of my strength and my refuge is in God. Trust in him at all times you people, pour out your heart before him; God is a refuge for us.*

We have to know we can come to our Father God, because he will defend us in all things. He is our refuge in trouble, and he will help us when we call upon him in truth, in Jesus's name.

Our God will hear us when we call upon him. Look at Psalm 63:1 which says: *O God thou art my God, early will I seek thee, my soul thirst for thee, my flesh long for thee in a dry and thirsty land where no water is.*

Psalm 64:1 says: *Hear my voice, O God in my prayer, preserve my life from fear of the enemy.*

Psalm 65:1 and 4 says: *Praise wait for thee, O God in Sion, and unto thee shall the vow be performed.* Verse 4 says: *Blessed is the man whom thou chooses and causes to approach unto thee, that he may dwell in thy courts, we shall be satisfied with the goodness of thy house even of thy holy temple.* Amen.

We can find out much about keeping a healthy spiritual heart recovered by the word of God; it is the best spiritual medicine for a painful, wounded heart in all its heart ailments and any spiritual heart attack.

God's desire is for our whole heart to be surrendered, vessels with clean hearts, with the word of God in our mouths and the meditation of our hearts will be acceptable in his sight according to Psalm 19:14. The Lord God will hear us in all our trouble, circumstances and situations. Psalm 20:1-2 says: *The Lord hear thee in the day of trouble, the name of the God of Jacob defend thee. Send thee help from the sanctuary and strengthen thee out of Zion Amen.*

As we study the scriptures and let them be birthed in our spirits we will grow more in the things of God and die to the things of this world; like status quo, name dropping, titles and positioning ourselves in positions God has not positioned us in.

Romans 6:11-14 says: *Likewise reckon ye also yourselves to be dead indeed unto sin, but alive unto God through Jesus Christ our Lord. Let not sin therefore reign in your mortal body, that ye should obey it in the lusts thereof. Neither yield ye your members as instruments of unrighteousness unto sin but yield yourselves unto God as those that are alive from the dead, and your members as instruments of righteousness unto God. For sin shall not have dominion over you, for ye are not under the law but under grace.*

As you adapt to these God-breathed words it will help you to continue to allow the Spirit of God and the Holy Spirit with Jesus to keep your spiritual heart under the assignment of taking inventory of how to keep a recovered spiritual heart in Jesus's name, Amen.

No matter what my circumstances have been, making the right decisions through the words of God and using it for problem solving and many solutions to every situation, believing and receiving truth from the word and standing on its promises has made a difference. God has proven himself to be faithful and he has kept every promise to me and some

I am awaiting for their manifestation with great expectation. I have learned many people, saved or unsaved, put their trust in money more than in the God of the universe. Their values are mixed up. Money will not buy them good health or real happiness, for what does it profit a man or woman to gain the world and their souls be lost forever?

My strength of consistency has caused and is causing me to stay on track spiritually; with the desire of God's Kingdom in my heart to satisfy my inner soul and spirit brings me much joy and peace. It fulfills and energizes my spirit, longing to please the Father of all creation. I now have a deeper understanding of who God has chosen me to be in him through discipline, taking action, being productive, studying to be quiet and still, listening to the still small voice of the Holy Spirit, completing the task ahead by looking unto Jesus, the author and finisher of my faith, having better organizational skills in all things by identifying goals to assist me with day to day tasks and skills. Phyllis is learning to be a better listener to others, not taking on other problems, and knowing I am not the savior of anyone's problem, just a vessel of The Savior Jesus Christ.

I have come to know what it means to be sober minded and alert; because there is an enemy of our minds, spirit and soul. He is called the thief, the killer and the destroyer; his name is the devil, Satan, Lucifer, the dragon, and the deceiver.

In 1 Peter 5:7-9, we find out how we can defeat this enemy of our souls. In my learning how to guard my heart and mind, the Holy Spirit has taught me how to cast the whole of my cares, concerns, worries, and anxieties on the Lord Jesus Christ by faith.

Let's have a little Bible teaching on this chapter and verses through the power of the Holy Spirit, who is the teacher helping us to rightly divide the word of truth.

1 Peter 5:7 says according to the amplified version: *Casting the whole of your care (all your anxieties, all your worries, all your concerns, once and for all on him, for he cares for you affectionately and cares about you watchfully.* Jesus is our caretaker who wants the whole of everything that concerns us. Nothing is too small or too simple that he is

willing to take it away and give us rest and peace within our hearts and minds.

1 Peter 5:8 says: *Be well balanced (temperate, sober of a sober mind), for that enemy of yours, the devil roams around like a lion roaring in fierce hunger, seeking someone to seize upon and devour.*

Verse 9: *We are to withstand him, be firm in faith against his onset rooted, established, strong, immovable, and determined, knowing that the same identical sufferings are appointed to your brotherhood (the whole body of Christians throughout the world.*

We, as believers, must stand strong in our faith against the onsets of the kingdom of darkness, be established in the power of Jesus Christ's power and might, be immovable, determined to be rooted in the word of God, settled always, abounding in the work of the Kingdom, standing on the solid foundation of the Living word of God which is Jesus our Savior, King of kings and Lord of lords, established and transformed in his image and likeness, Amen.

We are in a spiritual war as soldiers in the army of our God. We must fight the good fight of faith, according to 1 Timothy 6:12: *Our weapons for this warfare is not carnal but mighty through God through the pulling down of strongholds in Jesus's name.*

According to 2 Corinthians 10:5 *casting down imaginations and every high thing that exalt itself against the knowledge of God.* When we bring all our thoughts into the will and obedience to Christ Jesus, remember every thought comes from what is in our hearts. If the word is rooted deep down in our hearts, we can overcome anything on this Christian journey. Amen.

There are Kingdom strategies to use in spiritual warfare that are affected in this spiritual battle that gives us the victory; in Jesus's name, we win.

To be alert in the spirit realm is to wake up out of a deep sleep. It is now time to be soldiers of the Mighty God of heaven and earth. To be alert means to be keen in sound, in thought and mind, to be watchful, stay wide awake, in movement, ready to act and speak the word of God by faith.

We must be prepared for any attack from the enemy, praying in the spirit of the Holy Spirit, standing steadfast on the word and in faith. We must be vigilant to study, be watchful, giving warning, and being on guard of any approaching danger or harm from our enemy, the devil. Always being sober minded with temperance, not drunk with the cares of the world system, resisting the devil, being committed to God's Kingdom and the building of his Kingdom on earth as it is in heaven. To resist means to act on the word of God against the attack of the kingdom of darkness in the name of Jesus, by the blood of Jesus, Amen.

Our entire armor of God is to fight the fight of good faith as a good soldier, who can endure hardness as good soldiers in God's army. As we study, Ephesians 6:10-17 says: *Finally, my brother be strong in the Lord and in the power of his might.*

Verse 11: Put on the whole armour of God that you may be able to stand against the wiles of the devil.

Verse 12: For we wrestle not against flesh and blood, but against principalities, rulers of the darkness of this world, against spiritual wickedness in high places.

Verse 13: Wherefore take the shield of faith, wherewith ye shall be able to quench all the fiery darts of the wicked. Take unto you the whole amour of God that ye may be able to withstand in the evil day, and having done all to stand.

Verse 14: Stand therefore having your loins girt about with truth and having on the breastplate of righteousness.

Verse 15: And your feet shod with the preparation of the gospel of peace.

Verse 16: Above all, taking the shield of faith, wherewith ye shall be able to quench all the fiery darts of the wicked.

Verse 17: And take the helmet of salvation, and the sword of the Spirit, which is the word of God.

When we learn our warfare isn't against one another, but against principalities, powers, rulers of the darkness of this world and spiritual wickedness in high places, we can take our rightful positions at the direction of God through the Holy Spirit.

This is another way to guard our hearts and keep them recovered from any spiritual heart alignment. When we know that each brother or sister in the army of our God isn't the real enemy, we must understand the spirit behind each individual will either be of God or of the kingdom of darkness, to get victory over our enemies in Jesus's name, Amen.

As we commit ourselves to the Lord God, resisting our foe the devil, watching and seeing the salvation of God, we need to always watch and pray, asking God to keep our focus on the mark of the prize. As we have learned how to recover our Spiritual Heart from a Spiritual Heart Attack, let us learn to keep inventory of all our spiritual heart ailments, so that we can keep our hearts under the microscope of God's word that washes and cleanses us from all unrighteousness. As we learn to confess and meditate on the word of God by faith, the word will be hidden in our hearts and we can take a medicine in our spiritual hearts that works healing to all our spirits, soul, minds and bodies in Jesus's name, Amen.

Through the word and prayer, we can learn that meditation strengthens our communication with the Father God through the word (which is Jesus) and the power of the Holy Spirit.

These are some prescriptions that will be spiritual heart exercises.

Words of Confession to Keep Our Hearts under the Microscope of God's Word:

Psalm 5:3 says: *In the morning you hear my voice, O Lord: in the morning I prepare a prayer, a sacrifice for you and watch and wait for you to speak to my heart.*

Psalm 141:1-2 says: *Lord, I call upon you, hasten to me, give ear to my voice when I cry to you. Let my prayer be set forth as incense before you, the lifting up of my hands as the evening sacrifice.*

Psalm 142:1-2 says: *I cry to the Lord with my voice with my voice to the Lord do I make supplication.*

Psalm 143:1 says: *Hear my prayer, O Lord, give ear to my supplications! In your faithfulness, answer me, and in your righteousness.* Verse 2 says: *and enter not into judgement with your servant, for in your sight no man living is in himself righteous or justified.*

Philippians 4:4-8 says: *Rejoice in the Lord always and again I say rejoice. Let your moderation be known unto all men, the Lord is at hand. Be careful for nothing, but in everything by prayer and supplication with thanking let your, shall keep your hearts and minds through Jesus Christ.*

2 Corinthians 10:4 says: *the weapons of my warfare are not carnal but mighty through God to the pulling down of strongholds.*

Isaiah 54:14 says: *No weapon formed against me shall prosper, and every tongue that rises against me in judgement I condemn.*

I take the shield of faith and I quench every fiery dart of the enemy. (Ephesians 6:16)

I am redeemed from the curse of the law. I am redeemed from poverty, I am redeemed from sickness, I am redeemed from spiritual death. (Galatians 6:14-17)

I overcome all because greater is he that is in me than he that is in the world. (1 John 4:4)

I stand in the evil day having my loins girded about with truth, and I have the breastplate of righteousness. My feet are shod with the gospel of peace. I take the shield of faith, I am covered with the helmet of salvation, and I used the sword of the Spirit, which is the word of God. (Ephesians 6:14-17)

I am delivered from the power of darkness and translated into the Kingdom of God's dear Son. (Colossians 1:13)

I tread upon serpents and scorpions and over all the power of the enemy, and nothing shall hurt me. (Luke 10:19)

I am healed by the stripes of Jesus. (Isaiah 53:5)

As we have given you these scriptures to help assist you in keeping your healing to all the areas of our spiritual heart and all the ailments of our spiritual hearts, when we use them it will work healing to all our spirits, minds, and souls, even our bodies.

This book was written to bring healing for our spiritual heart from a spiritual heart attack and any spiritual heart ailments that will affect us in the spirit and in our natural bodies.

Please allow the Lord God and the Holy Spirit to minister to your spirit man and cause you to grow up spiritually in Christ Jesus our Lord.

As we journey through this life as believers, keep alert, trusting, believing, standing strong in the Lord and the power of his might, walking in faith and the love of God in Christ Jesus; know that God will keep you and lead you into all truth. As we keep pressing into his presence with a surrendered, yielding, committed, and sold out heart, we will come up to new levels of spirituality.

May the Lord God keep and make his face to shine upon you is my prayer.

This is my prayer for all who will purchase this book:

Father God, my prayer for each reader is that you will enlighten their eyes and mind of understanding, to know the depth, the length, and the breadth of your Spirit. I cease not to give thanks for you, making mention of you in my prayers. The God of our Lord Jesus the Father of glory may give unto you the spirit of wisdom and revelation in the knowledge of him. The eyes of your understanding being enlightened, that ye may know what is the hope of your calling and what the riches of the glory of his inheritance in the saints. Amen

P.S. May you Recover your love for God and his word that you may be the one he is calling to give his heartbeat to for Kingdom business and Kingdom enlightenment through Revelation knowledge and Truth in Jesus's name.

www.ingramcontent.com/pod-product-compliance
Lightning Source LLC
Chambersburg PA
CBHW070537010526
44118CB00012B/1153